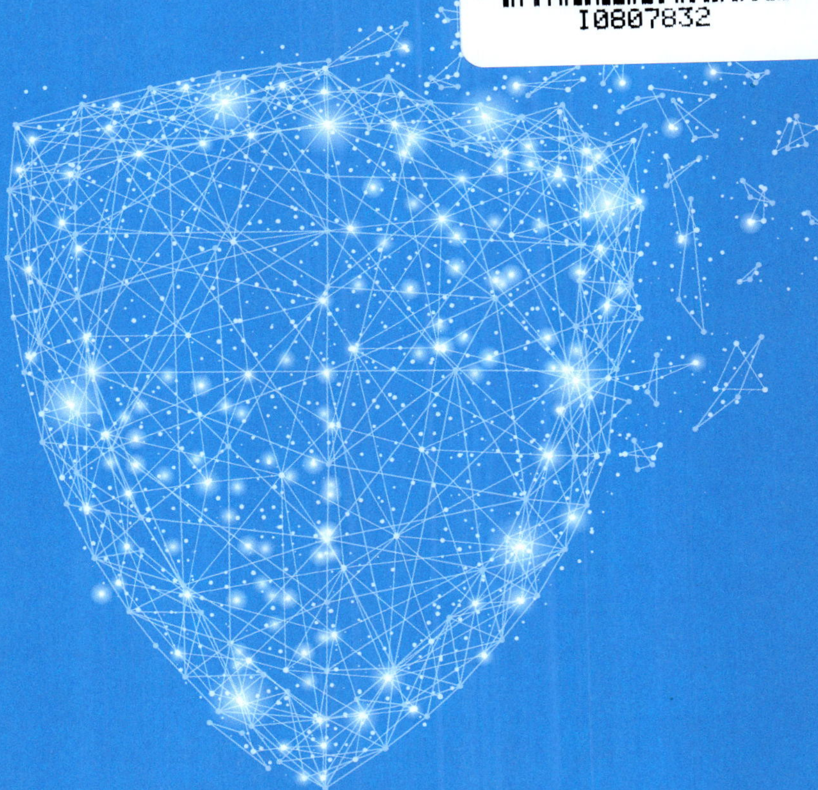

Preschool Preparedness for an Active Shooter

ANDREW ROSZAK,
JD, MPA, EMT-P

Gryphon House

Published by Gryphon House, Inc.
P. O. Box 10, Lewisville, NC 27023
800.638.0928; 877.638.7576 [fax]
Visit us on the web at www.gryphonhouse.com.

Library of Congress Control Number: 2019950530

Bulk Purchase

Gryphon House books are available for special premiums and sales promotions as well as for fund-raising use. Special editions or book excerpts also can be created to specifications. For details, call 800.638.0928.

Disclaimer

Gryphon House, Inc., cannot be held responsible for damage, mishap, or injury incurred during the use of or because of activities in this book. Appropriate and reasonable caution and adult supervision of children involved in activities and corresponding to the age and capability of each child involved are recommended at all times. Do not leave children unattended at any time. Observe safety and caution at all times.

Table of Contents

Acknowledgments

This publication would not be possible without the contributions of numerous individuals. First, we must acknowledge those brave individuals who have lived through the unthinkable. Our thoughts are with them and their families as they continue to recover from these senseless tragedies.

Second, a very special thank you to my father, Ronald Roszak, for his relentless work on this topic. As an award-winning law enforcement veteran with twenty years of service, his insights and contributions offer a unique perspective on this topic. Since day one, his passion for protecting children by empowering early childhood professionals has been awe inspiring. It has truly been a privilege to work alongside my father and travel the country with him to help better prepare individuals and organizations.

Third, I would be remiss if I did not acknowledge the many contributions of Dr. Sara Roszak. Sara has been the best wife, friend, and copyeditor anyone could possibly wish for. Without her support and encouragement, I certainly would not be where I am today.

Fourth, many thanks to Bob and Joyce Plechaty, Ruth Roszak, Amy Roszak, Joan Roszak, Maria Rubin, Dr. Kathy Morgan, and Marty Rubin for their love, inspiration, and encouragement.

Last, but certainly not least, I would like to thank all the early childhood professionals who have contributed to this work and those who are taking the time to read this publication. When I began working in early childhood in 2015, I was unsure what type of reception my work would receive—especially considering the multitude of competing interests and requirements that merit their time and attention. I have been beyond delighted and impressed that so many have embraced emergency preparedness and have moved beyond just checking the box. Your creativity, imagination, and dedication to keeping children safe is inspirational and is the driving force behind this work. I hope the following pages provide you with context, ideas, and useable solutions. It is an honor to stand beside you and work on these issues together.

Introduction

The Reasons for This Book

In the years leading up to this publication, the United States has endured numerous active-shooter incidents. The uptick in these tragic events has led to increased rules and regulations across states for specific entities, such as public institutions, to plan and train for responding to such scenarios. More recently, several states have enacted or are considering such regulations specifically for early childhood programs.

Recent research by Kendall Leser, Julie Looper-Coats, and Andrew Roszak relates that out of a sample of more than 600 child-care administrators nationwide, only 20 percent reported preparedness as a high-level priority for their child-care business. In this same study, when asked how prepared they were for various emergency situations, less than half of child-care administrators reported being prepared for an active shooter situation, while more than 90 percent reported being prepared for a fire. This finding makes sense given that child-care providers have been required to participate in fire drills for years, but not many providers have been required to prepare for and practice for active-shooter scenarios.

Given these new and proposed regulations requiring shooter/lockdown plans and conducting drills on a regular basis—and based on the concerns of early learning professionals—I have created this publication, the first of its kind, specifically tailored for the early learning community. This publication can serve as a starting point or review for early childhood professionals to empower themselves to address difficult and threatening situations.

Early Childhood Education: A Unique Setting

Preparing for an active-shooter scenario seems unimaginable to many—and even more so in the context of early education. At first, the thought of this type of preparation may be uncomfortable. After all, early childhood professionals care for the youngest and most vulnerable population: our children, the next generation. While many businesses, high schools, and universities have been preparing for shooter scenarios for years, the early childhood education community has largely been left out of such efforts. Sadly, this is not uncommon, as early childhood is often overshadowed or completely forgotten. There are many reasons for this, not the least of which is that people believe we are just "babysitters."

This could not be further from the truth.

Early childhood is an essential time in a child's life. Not only is the brain developing at an astonishing rate, but vital social, emotional, and sensory skills are being formed, all of which will have life-long impacts. According to the Center on the Developing Child at Harvard University, in children younger than three years, more than a million neural connections per second are being formed—more than at any other time of life. Our shared goal is to provide an environment that is nurturing, caring, healthy, and safe.

The challenge for us is balancing the security needs of our programs against the desire to ensure that our spaces are warm, open, and welcoming. It is not an easy task, especially considering that resources are often scarce in the early childhood setting. We attempt to balance these realities in the following pages, recognizing that child-care professionals are the first educators of emergency preparedness. Child-care providers are a foundational piece of emergency preparedness—and the reason why children already know what to do in emergencies when they reach elementary school.

Reading this publication is an important first step in your preparedness journey. The term *active shooter* is used throughout this publication for simplicity. However, the techniques described can be applied to a wide variety of situations and threats. For some, the term *active assailant* may be more appropriate. All of us hope that we will never find ourselves in a dangerous situation, especially one with a gunman. However, current realities underscore the importance of learning more about these scenarios and empowering ourselves with knowledge and the skills to prepare.

Currently, there is a gap between the threat that early childhood professionals may face and their level of preparedness to handle such scenarios. While the early learning community has a need for active-shooter planning, training, and education, few resources specifically address these unique environments, situations, and clientele.

DID YOU KNOW?

Every day in the United States, 69 million children under the age of eighteen are separated from their parents. These children are spending their time in child care, Head Start programs, school, or after-school programs (Hawa, 2014). That is about 20 percent of our nation's population, including 12 million children under the age of five (FEMA, 2019). That's a lot of kids and a lot of responsibility. But with proper training and planning, early childhood professionals can and do protect the children entrusted to their care.

By itself, reading this publication does not constitute being prepared. In addition, consider participating in classroom and hands-on training for this topic. That will truly help you put these concepts into practice. It is important, as well, to recognize the value of early mental-health and law enforcement intervention when parents, staff, or children display indicators that are worthy of immediate intervention.

The Basis of This Book

This publication is the culmination of countless hours of research, and it offers an important primer for early childhood professionals to become comfortable with the concept of preparing for an active-shooter scenario. To develop this publication, I examined real-world incidents, trained and engaged with early childhood professionals, conducted focus groups to better understand the needs of center-based and family-home-based providers, trained with first responders, conducted and participated in exercises, and worked with a multidisciplinary group of professionals. All these efforts took place with one goal in mind: to provide early childhood professionals with a written resource for how to begin preparing to deal with this very sensitive topic.

> **"I thought those people who worshipped [the killers] were sick and twisted, but I too am now going down that path. When the time comes I hope to outdo my idols and make my mark on the world just like they did."**
>
> —A fourteen-year-old active shooter who was successfully stopped and apprehended by a school resource officer after opening fire at a school in Socastee, South Carolina, in September 2010

This publication and the recommended strategies described within are grounded in real-world evidence, proven tactics, and strategies for responding to an active-shooter incident. Information is current as of the time of press; however, tactics and strategies to address these types of scenarios are constantly evolving. Often, active shooters have studied prior events to copy effective techniques and avoid ineffective ones. In turn, we must also be familiar with prior events to stay ahead of the curve and know how to react. Understanding prior events allows us to not only better respond to an incident, but in some cases, could also lead to preventing one from ever happening in the first place.

1 Background on the Threat

No one wants to find herself caught in the middle of an active-shooter scenario. Unfortunately, these scenarios can and do happen. Just as we prepare for hurricanes, floods, tornadoes, and earthquakes, we must also prepare for active-shooter events. In planning for all types of disasters, including active-shooter scenarios, special consideration must be taken for our most vulnerable population: children. Understanding what constitutes an active-shooter event and who perpetrates this type of crime is important for preparedness efforts. On its webpage "Active Shooter Resources," the Federal Bureau of Investigation (FBI) defines an *active shooter* as one or more individuals actively engaged in killing or attempting to kill people in a populated area. Unfortunately, there is not one profile that fits or predicts who might become an active shooter. Shooters have come in all ages, sexes, races, backgrounds, and religions. Even though each potential shooter is different, a review of historical events points to some similarities that the majority of these criminals share. Many active shooters believe that they will gain popularity and notoriety for their heinous acts, which is why we purposefully omit the names of these individuals in this publication.

Most active shooters share the following characteristics:

- Personal grievance
- Interest in prior shootings
- Prior encounters with law enforcement
- Personal connection with the location
- Preplanning of the attack
- Single individual

Mass shootings are typically not carried out on a whim. Instead, most shootings are preplanned, and a majority of the shooters actually have personal connections to the sites that they attack. However, rarely do they make plans to escape from the scene or location. The majority of attackers do not plan to escape but rather plan to be killed by law enforcement, to commit suicide, or to be apprehended. These traits and characteristics are important to keep in mind when we begin to plan our response.

Jillian Peterson of Hamline University and James Densley of Metropolitan State University report further data on school shooters:

- 91 percent are students or former students
- 87 percent were in crisis before the shooting
- 80 percent were suicidal prior to the shooting
- 78 percent leaked their plans ahead of time, usually on social media

Characteristics that drive active shooters are important to understand as we prepare. First and foremost, the shooters recognize that they have a limited amount of time to inflict harm on others. The shooters know they have to act quickly before they run out of ammunition or are confronted by law enforcement officials. Ultimately, their goal is to kill as many people they can, as quickly as possible.

Prior shooters have chosen locations with weak or little security, referred to as *soft targets*. They chose these places because they offered easy access to unprotected individuals. Much like other criminals, they looked for locations with doors that were unlocked, individuals who were not paying attention, or places that lacked security measures. During a majority of past shootings, the incidents concluded quickly when the shooters were faced with obstacles or resistance.

Up against the constraints of time, most active shooters choose victims at random. Shooters often look for quick and easy targets, leading them to choose locations with large populations: nightclubs, movie theaters, sporting events, concerts, and schools. In many cases, these locations were chosen not at random but for their high concentration of potential victims.

While it is certainly important to prepare for active-shooter incidents, it's also important to keep the threat in perspective. Active-shooter events are still relatively infrequent. As with all hazards that we prepare for, we must take into account the likelihood and probability of these events occurring.

According to FBI data, between 2000 and 2017 there were 250 mass shootings in the United States, killing a total of 799 people. For comparison, the Centers for Disease Control and Prevention (CDC) says that in any given year about 610,000 Americans die of heart disease. The fact is that we are much more likely to die from heart disease than from an active-shooter incident.

In any given year, according to the National Coalition Against Domestic Violence (NCADV), more than 10 million men and women in the United States are physically abused by an intimate partner. Intimate-partner violence accounts for 15 percent of all violent crime in this country. The effects of domestic violence are not confined to adults: One in fifteen children is exposed to such violence each year, and 90 percent of these children are eyewitnesses to the violence. Another type of violence that is a significant public health concern, according to Healthline, is suicide, the tenth-leading cause of death in the United States. Beyond violence and chronic disease, accidents or unintentional injuries are a leading health concern in the United States, especially for people ages one to forty-four. Accidents lead to 28 million emergency room visits each year and are the third-leading cause of death in this country.

We hear a lot about active-shooter incidents at schools, and our inclination is likely to think that children are more at risk than adults. However, when examining the odds of our children dying from an active-shooter incident, we see figures similar to those for adults. For example, students are 250 times more likely to die at home from domestic violence, 350 times more likely to die in a car wreck, and 150 times more likely to die from suicide than from an active-shooter incident (ChildTrends, 2019). So while it is important for students to be prepared and learn response techniques, the chance of dying from an active-shoot incident remains relatively low (Ropeik, 2018).

WHAT ARE THE ODDS?

According to the National Safety Council, an American's lifetime odds of dying in a mass shooting committed in any location are 1 in 11,125. For comparison, the odds of dying in a car accident are 1 in 491; of drowning, 1 in 1,133; of being struck by lightning, 1 in 3,000; and of choking on food, 1 in 3,461. The odds of a student being a victim of a school-associated shooting are 1 in 2.5 million.

These statistics are provided to give you some peace of mind. While it may seem like active-shooter events are happening very frequently, the likelihood of being involved in one of these situations is extremely low. As with all of our preparedness activities, we want to ensure we are aware of the scope and risk. The purpose of this book is not to cause anxiety or fear but to empower the reader through discussion of tools and techniques and an examination of leading practices for active-shooter response.

To summarize, active shooters are criminals with the intent to inflict harm or kill others, but they do not necessarily have a relationship to their target location. In the context of early childhood education, there could be people familiar with locations who plan to inflict harm. This could be an estranged parent, a disgruntled or recently fired employee, or even someone with ill intent toward children.

It is important to be discreet about sharing preparedness plans and about updating and revising those procedures. In the early childhood workforce, according to researcher Noriko Porter, each year we have a 30 percent national turnover rate. Employees, parents, and others come and go from child-care locations, and it's important to bear in mind that a small percentage of people could have ill intent.

Throughout this publication, we offer recommendations and strategies on how to address active-shooter scenarios, as well as provide examples from prior scenarios for context. As we've discussed, much can be learned from previous tragedies, and the goal is to stay one step ahead of potential future shooters. The shooters are reviewing and sometimes idolizing earlier tragedies. However, as child-care professionals look to prepare themselves and their facilities, these prior events can offer many lessons and opportunities to think differently about how to respond to such scenarios in the future.

2 Historical Lessons Learned

Our purpose in reviewing prior mass shootings is not to cast blame or second-guess decisions made by victims or first responders in the confusion and chaos of a situation. Rather, it is to learn from these incidents by examining what worked well and identifying areas for possible improvement. In all these events, it would not be fair to compare the information that we have today to the information available while an incident unfolded, as strategies and tactics have changed and continue to evolve. In all cases, we remember the heroes, the victims, and the families who are still suffering from these senseless tragedies.

Columbine High School, 1999

What Happened

Two students planned and executed an attack on their Littleton, Colorado, high school in 1999. The shooting occurred in April, not long after the school prom, and as the shooting unfolded, some people thought it might be a senior prank. Initially, the perpetrators planted two twenty pound propane bombs in the school cafeteria and planned to shoot at students and teachers fleeing from the inferno they hoped to create. However, their bombs failed to detonate; instead, they began their shooting spree and had to re-enter the school. In total, the shooters killed thirteen individuals and wounded twenty-four.

The *Report of Governor Bill Owens' Columbine Review Commission* relates that the shooters entered the school building while firing at students outside and continued shooting at people within the cafeteria. The first 911 call was made by a student reporting a woman down in the parking lot. Early in the shooting, the school custodian also notified the school's resource officer, who was a Jefferson County sheriff's deputy, to report trouble at the school. Many people either fled outside or took shelter in the library. The shooters reached the library about fifteen minutes into their shooting spree. A teacher made an emergency call to 911 from the library; gunfire and explosions can be heard from the hallway on the recording.

Following existing protocols, students were directed by staff and teachers to hide in the library under desks, as this was the policy for a lockdown situation. Sixty people were hiding in the library when the shooters arrived. Of the thirteen people killed, ten of them were killed in the library over the span of seven-and-a-half minutes.

While the lockdown procedures in classrooms likely saved many lives, today we would respond differently. Because these were high school students, today the preferred response would be to run and escape the danger. In 1999, however, there was neither training nor a focus on active-shooter response, and the lockdown in the library focused more on hiding under desks than securing and barricading doors or taking action against the shooters. The commission's report states that during the attack, "no efforts were made to engage, contain, or capture the perpetrators."

Law enforcement responded to the events at Columbine, and the first officer arrived on the scene within minutes of the beginning of the attack. Hearing gunshots, the first responding officer established a perimeter and requested that the Special Weapons and Tactics (SWAT) team respond. The first officers stayed outside of the building and did not allow anyone in or out of the area as they waited for SWAT to arrive. SWAT arrived on the scene approximately forty minutes later and then made entry into the building.

From the library, the shooters exchanged gunfire with police, moved to other areas in the school while shooting at people, and then turned their guns on themselves in a school office. They took their own lives forty-six minutes after their attack began, but first responders were unaware of this, so it was several more hours before the school was secured and medical attention was provided for those inside the school.

Lessons Learned

- Place emergency calls immediately or as soon as possible.
- Police should confront the shooter as quickly as possible.
- If possible, people inside the building should get out.
- If it is not possible to leave the building, people should hide and limit the shooter's access to the hiding place.

Reports vary, but it is generally agreed that there was a six- to eight-minute delay from the time of the first gunshots until the first 911 call was placed. This delay increased police response time and arguably cost lives. We need to ensure 911 (or the number used in your country) is called in a timely manner. This speaks to the topic of situational awareness, which we will explore in depth in chapter 4. If you see or hear things that are out of the ordinary, that make you feel unsafe or that you are threatened, call 911 without delay. The police would much rather respond and determine that your concerns are unfounded than have the emergency call delayed.

Law enforcement has realized that a surround-and-contain strategy is not the best approach in these incidents. *Surround and contain* is an approach typically used by law enforcement during a hostage situation. This approach may work in situations where innocent people are being held with the threat of being killed or injured. However, in an active-shooter situation, violence is already underway and more direct action is needed from law enforcement to end the shooting.

Further, in 1999 most law enforcement officers were armed with minimal weaponry—usually a handgun and a shotgun. When responding to active-shooter events, the first arriving officers would have been outmatched in weapons and firepower. They also would not have had access to such tactical tools and equipment as bulletproof shields, riot gear, and extra ammunition, which were, at the time, provided primarily to SWAT teams.

With these realities in mind, there has been a shift away from thinking of these incidents as hostage situations or situations that require a SWAT-team response. As a result of Columbine, police are now equipped with additional weaponry and other tools and resources they need to quickly respond to these incidents and are trained to enter a building and confront a shooter as quickly as possible, to prevent further injury and death.

Response plans need to account for the differences between a threat inside a building and a threat outside a building. For external threats, a process of securing the building, moving individuals away from exterior windows, and staying low is appropriate. For internal threats, when the source of danger is inside a building, bystanders should escape the building if possible. If escape is not possible, occupants should take steps to hide from the shooter and limit access to the occupants' space. These steps include shutting, locking, and barricading doors; covering windows; turning off lights; and staying as quiet as possible. For internal threats, occupants also want to prepare themselves for a possible confrontation with the shooter.

Virginia Tech, 2007

What Happened

The shooting at Virginia Polytechnic Institute and State University, commonly known as Virginia Tech, occurred in 2007. In this particular event, there were two shootings two hours apart. Thirty-two individuals were killed, making it the deadliest shooting in United States history at the time. CNN, in its article "Virginia Tech Shootings Fast Facts," relates that the first shooting occurred around 7:15 a.m. inside a women's residential dormitory. The shooter in this case was male. As such, he did not have permission to enter the women's dorms but gained access after someone held the door open for him. Once inside, he shot a female and a male.

More than two hours passed after the initial shooting took place before the school sent out an email statement that a shooting had taken place earlier that morning. During this time, the shooter was still on the loose. At the time, police believed the first shooting to be an isolated incident of domestic violence. Rachel Fretz, in her article "Lessons Learned at Virginia Tech Shooting" for PoliceOne.com, relates that police did not issue a warning to the campus or institute a campus lockdown because it was deemed unnecessary. For the other 131 buildings on campus, it was a normal day.

The shooter changed clothes and then worked his way across campus. He ended up in an educational building known as Norris Hall. The shooter locked and chained the first-floor doors shut using chains that he had brought with him in his backpack. In the span of eleven minutes, he shot forty-seven students, staff, and faculty. He then killed himself.

The shooter entered several classrooms, which is where most of the casualties occurred. Some classrooms had no notice of the event; others had a limited amount of time to prepare. As we look at the actions that were taken in this situation, we can see a marked difference in survivability. Three of the classrooms were able to take action and barricade their doors. The simple act of denying the shooter entry into the classroom led to a significant reduction in casualties.

When the shooting began, seventy-six-year-old professor Liviu Lirescu took action. *The Washington Post* reported that Professor Lirescu was a Holocaust survivor who had been teaching for more than twenty years. He ran to the classroom door, which could not be locked from the inside, and attempted to barricade it with his body. At the same time, he instructed his students to jump out of the window of the second-story classroom to safety. The shooter appeared and attempted to force his way into the classroom. A struggle ensued, and the shooter fired through the door four times, killing Professor Lirescu. By the time the shooter entered the classroom, all but one student had escaped through the window. Professor Lirescu's heroic actions saved the lives of twenty-two of his students.

Lessons Learned

- Warn others of a potentially dangerous situation immediately.
- Barricade doors with furniture, not with human beings.
- Cellular calls to the authorities should be routed appropriately.

The importance of warning others of a potentially dangerous situation is crucial. Advance warning allows time to take action. It also allows us to see the big picture. Had a campus-wide alert been issued, perhaps someone would have thought the chained doors of Norris Hall were suspicious and would have reported them. Instead, students assumed the doors were chained due to construction, and they entered Norris Hall through an open window nearby. Similarly, the initial noise of shots being fired led some students to dismiss them as construction noise. The importance of our situational awareness can't be overstated.

After the shooting, a number of lawsuits were filed against the university. Parents charged that the university should have warned students and initiated a campus-wide lockdown. The U.S. Department of Education issued a fine against the university under the Clergy Act, which requires universities to provide timely warnings of threats to students and staff. The legal challenges lasted for years and, by one estimate, cost the university upwards of $48.2 million. These consequences are an important reminder of the corollary issues that can present themselves after an incident is over.

The actions of Professor Lirescu were heroic. His swift action made a difference and saved lives. However, we can learn from this incident about the dangers of barricading a door with our bodies. First, we can find ourselves in a battle of strength as both parties try to control the door. Second, the obvious danger of standing behind a door is that a shooter can shoot through the door. For these two reasons, it is preferable to use tables, chairs, desks, bookshelves, and other furniture as barricades. In applying this lesson, we must arrange our classrooms in a way that makes barricading as quick and easy as possible.

Rachel Fretz relates that the first 911 call to alert the campus police of the shooting in Norris Hall was made from a cellular phone. The call was routed to a nearby police department due to the location of the cell phone tower. The local police dispatcher was not familiar with Norris Hall and transferred the call back to campus police. As reported in *Mass Shootings at Virginia Tech* by the Virginia Tech Review Panel, another cellular phone call from inside the building was routed to the Montgomery County, Virginia, sheriff dispatch instead of campus police. Because of these technical issues, the law enforcement response was delayed. (We will discuss making emergency calls from cell phones in more detail in chapter 5.)

The events at Virginia Tech reemphasize the need for timely notice and communication. Ultimately in these situations, individuals need to be provided notice of the active-shooter incident so that they can quickly take action and protect themselves.

Sandy Hook Elementary School, 2012

What Happened

According to the after-action report by the Connecticut State Police, on December 14, 2012, the shooter shot his mother at their home in Newtown, Connecticut. Neighbors heard the shots but assumed they were from hunters and did not report them to the police. After killing his mother, the shooter drove to Sandy Hook Elementary School.

Around 9:30 a.m., the shooter arrived at the school. Per policy, the external doors to the school were locked. The shooter shot out one of the lobby doors at the front of the school to gain entry and was immediately confronted by the principal, the school psychologist, and a teacher. The shooter killed the principal and psychologist and wounded the teacher. He then entered the front office, where the staff had effectively hidden. Seeing no one in the front office, the shooter walked down the hall toward the first-grade classrooms.

The first classroom he approached belonged to teacher Kaitlin Roig. When the shooting started, she took immediate action. She rushed her fifteen students into the classroom bathroom, barricaded the door, and kept the children quiet. The window in the door of her classroom was already covered from a prior lockdown drill. During the event, Ms. Roig kept the children calm and provided reassurance to them. The shooter bypassed her room completely, possibly thinking the classroom was vacant. Everyone in Ms. Roig's classroom survived.

The shooter proceeded down the hallway and eventually entered two first-grade classrooms. In these classrooms, the shooter killed eighteen first graders and four adults, including a substitute teacher. During the chaos, nine children ran from the classroom; they all survived. Two children hid in the classroom restroom, and they survived as well. Two wounded children would later be pronounced dead at the hospital. The shooter then committed suicide as police were entering the building.

The entire incident lasted approximately eight minutes and left twenty children and six adults dead.

During the incident, staff and students in other areas of the building hid and attempted to keep quiet. Some teachers had the children color pictures or read books to keep them calm and quiet. Once the shooting was over and the police had entered the school, they began going classroom to classroom. This procedure enables law enforcement personnel to determine whether any other threats exist and helps them locate survivors and those in need of medical attention. When the police knocked on Ms. Roig's bathroom door, she refused to open it. She requested that police slide their badges under the door. She also questioned why the police did not have the key. In fact, the police did have a key, but it was on a janitor's key ring with multiple other keys.

Lessons Learned

- Doors should be lockable from inside the classroom.
- Substitute teachers should be trained on emergency procedures and policies and should be issued classroom keys.
- Schools should maintain accurate daily attendance records. These should be easily accessible in the event of an emergency.
- When you hide, stay put and do not open the door for anyone. Law enforcement will come to you after the incident is over.
- It is helpful to engage with first responders before an event. That way, they are more familiar with your building layout, operating hours, and emergency plans.
- Alert authorities to a person who is showing signs of potentially hurting others.

After the shooting, the governor of Connecticut established the Sandy Hook Advisory Commission. The commission spent two years reviewing the incident, listening to testimony from experts, and reviewing laws, policies, and practices. Based on this work, the commission developed a set of recommendations aimed at reducing or preventing future tragedies.

The commission identified door locks as an area for improvement. The doors at Sandy Hook Elementary School were able to be locked only from outside the classroom. This policy prevented a timely response, as teachers would have to leave the safety of their classrooms and enter the hallway to lock the doors. The commission recommended that doors be lockable from the inside. Also, as noted above, a substitute teacher, Lauren Rousseau, was working at Sandy Hook Elementary school and was killed during the shooting. Her death serves as an important reminder that we must ensure substitute teachers receive proper training in emergency procedures and policies and also be issued the necessary keys to secure classroom doors.

The actions taken by Ms. Roig were indeed heroic. Undoubtedly her actions saved lives. The children followed her lead that day and stayed calm and quiet thanks to her actions and demeanor. What we learn from Ms. Roig is that having a plan, quickly taking action, staying calm, and being a source of strength for the children can make the difference between life and death. By refusing to open the door when the police arrived, Ms. Roig underscores an important point: The police will come to you once the event is over. Your best course of action is to stay put and not open the door for anyone until they show identification.

Many law enforcement agencies have moved away from issuing metal badges in favor of sewn-on badges and/or more tactical uniforms, making it less likely that a responding officer will be able to slide identification under the door. In response to this change in uniform, several law enforcement agencies are currently developing identification cards that they will use to slide under the door in these types of situations. Such a change would allow personnel to quickly identify that they are indeed communicating with the real police.

We frequently hear the phrase, "See something, say something." According to the report to the Office of the Child Advocate of the state of Connecticut, the shooter in this case had a long and detailed history of mental-health problems. As a fifth grader, he had created a notebook full of disturbing thoughts. He also created a spreadsheet that ranked prior mass shootings. In the notebook, he would write episodes of "Dora the Beserker," an obvious play on the popular children's television show of a similar name. In one of the shooter's imagined episodes, "Dora" asks another character to kill a soldier, to which she replies, "I like hurting people . . . especially children." Later in the episode, Dora sends "Swiper the Raccoon" into a child-care center to distract the children, then enters and says, "Let's hurt children." This represents the first direct evidence we have of an active shooter potentially contemplating hurting children in a child-care setting.

As tragic as the Sandy Hook shooting was, it could have been much worse. There were some true heroes who made a difference in the overall outcome and limited the total number of fatalities in this incident. First, the principal and psychologist took immediate action and ran toward the shooter. Their action alerted others of the situation and gave them a chance to hide, particularly those in the front office. As will be discussed in chapter 5, challenging the shooter is not necessarily a bad thing. However, we need to think about what tools we can have to help level the playing field. Had the principal or psychologist attacked the shooter with a fire extinguisher, for example, perhaps the situation would have turned out differently.

Often we think of active shooters as being insurmountable foes. However, the shooter in this incident was a little over six feet tall and weighed 112 pounds. Most adults would have a good chance of being able to overpower a person of that weight, especially if coupled with the benefit of an improvised weapon and the advantage of surprise.

Second, the quick actions of Ms. Roig serve as an excellent example of how implementing effective hiding strategies—turning off lights, barricading doors, and keeping people calm and quiet—can save lives. Ms. Roig and the other teachers at Sandy Hook who acted calmly and kept their students quiet with activities and reassurance did a superb job of responding to this crisis.

Third, the actions of some of the students in the two first-grade classrooms, particularly the nine children who ran and the two who hid in the bathroom, illustrate the different outcomes possible in active-shooter situations. The children ran and they hid, and in this case, both approaches worked well for these students. All eleven of these children survived.

Marjory Stoneman Douglas High School, 2018

What Happened

According to the *Initial Report Submitted to the Governor, Speaker of the House of Representatives, and Senate President* from the Marjory Stoneman Douglas High School Public Safety Commission (MSD PSC), in February 2018 fourteen students and three staff members were killed at Stoneman Douglas High School in Parkland, Florida. Another seventeen were wounded during the attack. The shooter was a former student of the high school who struggled with behavioral health issues.

At 2:19 p.m., the shooter arrived at the school via an Uber. As he exited the car, he was carrying a large duffel bag that contained a rifle and several hundred rounds of ammunition. He was able to enter the school campus via an unlocked and unstaffed security gate. He then proceeded to the north side of the campus, eventually approaching Building 12, which he entered through an unlocked and unstaffed door.

Inside Building 12, the shooter shot and injured thirty-four individuals. He never entered a single classroom but shot at students in the hallway or shot into classrooms through the windows of the classroom doors. The concussion from the shooting caused dust to fall from the ceiling tiles in the building and triggered the fire alarm. The alarm caused additional confusion, as many students began evacuating in a calm manner under the assumption that this was just a fire drill. Additionally, the fire-alarm noise masked the sound of some of the gunshots.

As reported in the South Florida *Sun-Sentinel*, at the time the fire alarm was activated, the shooter was on the first floor of the building. Those on the first floor lacked time to react to the unfolding events. Meanwhile, on the third floor, students and teachers could not distinctly hear gunshots and did not realize a shooter was in their midst, so students were evacuated from their classrooms and into the hall in response to the sound of the fire alarm. The third floor was described as being "packed with students, shoulder-to-shoulder." The shooter then moved to the second floor of the building, where students were hiding in classrooms that were made to look unoccupied. Students and teachers on the second floor had distinctly heard gunshots on the first floor and rapidly had hidden in their classrooms, making the floor look completely unoccupied. The shooter reportedly made statements such as, "No one is here," and began looking for additional targets. As a result, no shots were fired on the second floor and no deaths recorded.

Luckily, one of the teachers on the third floor had heard the shooting on the first floor and began telling students to head back into their classrooms. However, some students were unable to do so, as the classroom doors were equipped with mechanisms that automatically locked once someone exited the classroom. The teacher struggled to locate his keys to unlock the doors.

At this point, the shooter had arrived on the third floor. Approximately twenty students still remained in the third-floor hallway. The shooter quickly shot ten of these individuals, as well as two teachers who were holding their classroom doors open for students.

The individuals remaining in the hallway scattered for cover. A few students attempted to take shelter inside the bathrooms. However, those doors had been locked in an effort to curtail the number of students vaping in the bathrooms. The teacher who had been looking for his keys changed locations and attempted to enter through another classroom door. That door was locked as well. Seeing no other options, the teacher waited until the shooter was reloading his rifle and then sprinted with ten students toward the stairwell. Eight of the ten students successfully reached it; two were shot within feet of the stairwell.

The teacher then barricaded the stairwell door. The shooter attempted to gain entry to the stairwell but was unsuccessful. Approximately one-and-a-half minutes later, the shooter fired his last shot.

He then put down his weapon and exited the building, eventually blending in with the other students who were escaping. He roamed about the community, stopping at a Walmart, a Subway restaurant, and a McDonald's. He ordered a soft drink at Subway and sat down at a table inside the McDonald's with another high school student. Unbeknownst to the student, his sister had been shot by the shooter a short time earlier.

The shooter then exited the restaurant and spent the next thirty-five minutes walking through the community. He was captured by the police one hour and sixteen minutes after the first shots were fired, approximately two miles southwest of the high school.

Lessons Learned

- Security is effective only if it is monitored.
- Doors should be lockable from within the classroom.
- Doors should not automatically lock when someone leaves the classroom.
- Know which doors can be accessed and which cannot. Have keys readily available to unlock doors as needed in an emergency.
- Take all drills seriously and ensure staff and students are calm and quiet.
- Security cameras should show what is happening in real time and be recording at all times.
- Create or obtain window coverings that can be quickly applied to cover classroom windows.
- Identify hard corners where people could hide from a shooter. Clear anything that prevents access.

- Communication is essential. Provide means of communication between classrooms and the office, including a public-address system, walkie-talkies, intercoms, and telephones, and train staff on how to use them.
- Provide a back-up means of communication, such as air horns. Train staff on when and how to use them.
- Train all staff on what to do in an emergency. Ensure they know that they have the authority to call 911 (or the emergency number in your country) or to announce that there is imminent danger.
- Use plain language, instead of code words, when communicating in an emergency.

At the time of the shooting, the school had 3,318 enrolled students. Officials had spent a lot of time, resources, and money to ensure the school was a secure facility, including installing parking-lot and pedestrian gates. The school campus was also surrounded by a six-foot-high fence. Unfortunately, as dismissal time for the day grew closer, the security began to get lax.

Around 2:15 p.m., the parking-lot and pedestrian gates were opened and left unattended to help prepare for the 2:40 p.m. dismissal. These end-of-day preparations provided an opportunity for the shooter, who arrived at 2:19 p.m. and entered through an open, unstaffed pedestrian gate. When the shooter approached Building 12, he found those doors unlocked and unattended as well, as per the existing policy for the high school.

As previously noted, the bathrooms on the first and third floors of the building were locked to deter students from vaping in the bathrooms. The second-floor bathroom was open and was monitored by a staff member. During the shooting, several students attempted to seek refuge in the third-floor bathroom, only to encounter a locked door. This shortcoming highlights an important part of preparation: Know which doors you can and cannot access in the facility.

Just as we saw six years prior in Sandy Hook, the classroom doors here could be locked only from the outside, forcing teachers to leave the safety of their classrooms to go into the hallways and lock their doors. The mechanism that locked the door when someone exited the classroom also locked staff and students out of the classroom.

The activation of the fire alarm caused great confusion. As is typical during a fire alarm, students and staff exited the classrooms and went into the hallways. Video footage suggests that students were not taking the fire alarm seriously and continued to talk and joke with each other during the incident. This serves as an important reminder to take all drills seriously and to ensure staff and students are calm and quiet.

Cameras are an important part of any security strategy. When the police arrive, they will want to have access to the camera system so that they can see what is happening. The large forty-five-acre campus of Marjory Stoneman Douglas High School was equipped with numerous video cameras, including thirteen in Building

12 alone. However, none of these cameras captured the shooter's arrival at the high school, and many of them were motion activated and thus did not record anything when no movement was occurring. Unfortunately, the police did not learn until later that the system at the high school was on delay. According to the MSD PSC, some reports have indicated that this delay could have been as long as twenty-six minutes. As a result, law enforcement officials were always working from a deficit, as they could not see in real time what was happening.

As noted previously, the shooter never gained access to any of the classrooms; he shot victims in his line of sight and shot at others through the windows in the classroom doors. This highlights two points: the need to create or obtain window coverings that can be quickly applied to cover classroom windows and the importance of identifying hard corners. A *hard corner* is an area of a room or classroom that allows someone to hide—an area of the room that is not visible when someone attempts to look through the door window. Unfortunately, many classrooms had obstructions that prevented staff and students from accessing existing hard corners. Bookshelves, desks, computers, boxes, and other items prevented access to these areas. It is important to identify these areas ahead of time and ensure they are free from obstructions, even if that means moving classroom furniture.

Communication during this chaotic situation was difficult. Staff faced numerous challenges and lacked effective resources to communicate with the main office from classrooms. Also, public-address systems were not installed in all parts of the building, and very few staff members were issued radios. Furthermore, the announcement alerting the school to the presence of an active shooter was not made until after the shooter had shot all of his victims. When the announcement was made, instead of plain language, administrators used "Code Red," a term that led to additional confusion because the staff was unfamiliar with what a Code Red was. When communicating during an emergency, plain language, helps eliminate confusion and allows all individuals to be notified of exactly what the emergency is. Once a shooter is on the loose, there is not much good in trying to mask the reality of the situation by using code words. It is best to use plain language such as, "There is an active shooter in the hallway, and he is approaching the third-grade classroom." Using plain language ensures all individuals are receiving accurate information that enables and empowers them to act appropriately.

Communication will likely always be difficult in an emergency. Traditional communication methods may fail, either due to overuse or a lack of power or a lack of knowledge on how to use the intercom or phone system. Identifying simple and easy-to-use backup options is a leading practice. One simple option is to install an air horn in each classroom. Air horns are cheap, easy to use, and very loud. Under this strategy, all staff would be trained on how to use an air horn—and instructed that it is to be used only in the event of an active-shooter incident.

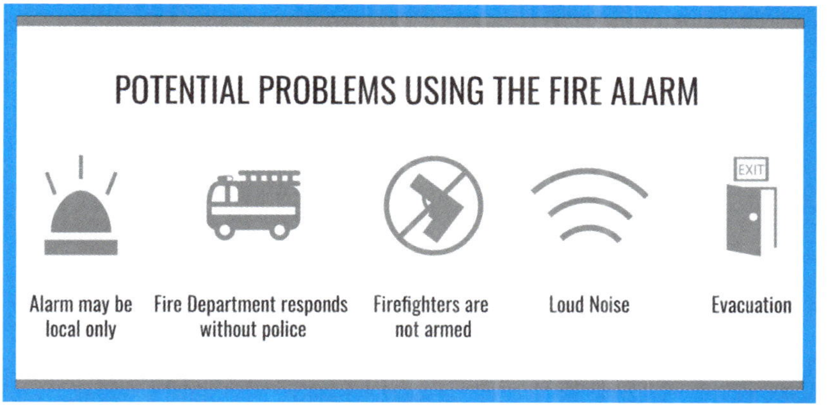

The principal of the school was very familiar with the day-to-day operations, having served as assistant principal for twelve years before being promoted to principal. At the time of the shooting, he had been principal for six years. However, on the day of the shooting, the principal was not on-site. This fact is important for a variety of reasons. First, it underscores the importance of ensuring all staff are trained in emergency procedures. Second, many of the teachers reported that they were unsure who could begin the notification of an active-shooter event. Some believed that they lacked the authority to do so and thought that only an administrator could make the announcement. In such situations, everyone must have the authority to call 911 (or the emergency number in your country) and make an announcement about imminent danger.

In the next chapter, we will explore how to apply the lessons learned in these tragedies to typical early childhood facilities.

3

Applying the Lessons Learned to Early Childhood Facilities

The purpose of recounting the history of prior active-shooter events is to learn from them and understand how to apply those lessons to prepare for such scenarios in the early childhood setting. Over the years, the approaches used to best prepare for active-shooter events have evolved, and much has been learned from challenges and successes in prior responses. Here are some key takeaways from those events that can inform our own preparedness in the early childhood setting.

Notification

As we learned from the Virginia Tech incident, notification is key. Unfortunately, many child-care programs are not receiving notifications or alerts from their local jurisdictions. Often, child-care programs are notified of a nearby incident because parents have one child in child care and an older child in the local school system. When parents receive an alert from the school, they will often call the child-care program to make them aware.

Child-care programs are encouraged to reach out to their local jurisdictions to learn what type of emergency alert and notifications are in place. Several communities and fifteen state-wide alerting systems use a program called CodeRED, a service provided by a company named OnSolve. An easy way to see what programs may be available for your location is to search the internet for emergency alerts in your city or county. These systems are often run by the local emergency-management agency or the police department.

If your community does not have a formal emergency-alert system, consider contacting the local school system. Several child-care programs have successfully established partnerships with their local school systems to share emergency information and alerts. However, these collaborations are unlikely to occur unless you reach out to the school system.

If neither of the above options is available to you, consider using 911 when you are concerned or feel that you need more information. For example, if you hear numerous sirens or see multiple police cars in your area, then you may want to call 911 and ask if the area is safe. The dispatcher is unlikely to provide you with detailed specifics regarding the incident, but if you explain that you have children at your facility and you are wondering if it is safe to be outside on the playground or to dismiss them to their parents, they will likely provide you with some guidance.

Staff Empowerment

An active-shooter event can happen at any time of day in any location. Often, child-care directors are off-site attending training or other meetings. Active-shooter events unfold within seconds and are often over in minutes. Staff need to be prepared and nimble so they can take the response into their own hands rather than being reactive or waiting for permission or direction. All staff need to be aware of what is expected of them and who is in charge in the event that the director is off-site.

As we saw from the incident in Parkland, Florida, the initial announcement may never come or may come too late. Child-care programs often allow parents access to the classrooms to pick up and drop off their children. If an incident were to start in a classroom, not in the front office, then we must ensure the teacher in that room knows she has the authority to alert others in the building. Therefore, all staff should be trained to call 911 (or the emergency number in your country) in emergency situations or when they feel unsafe, regardless of their rank or position within the organization. In many of the incidents we have examined, heroes emerged when individuals proactively took decisive action.

Locks and Access

As you have probably noted, many of these incidents happened due to lapses in security. Maintaining a secure environment is essential. This includes making sure exterior doors are locked and not propped open; discouraging *tailgating* (when an unauthorized person slips in through a door before it closes) and *piggybacking* (when an authorized person allows someone to follow him through a door to a secure area); questioning those who are attempting to enter your building; and enforcing access-control policies for parents and staff.

In addition, staff also need to be mindful of the access that they have inside the facility. This includes the areas they use to move children around inside the building, such as from the classroom to the playground, from lunch to the classroom, and so on. It is important that staff take note of which doors are locked, which doors they have a key to access, and which doors they do not have access to. In Parkland, Florida, several of the students tried to seek shelter inside a bathroom only to find that it was locked due to a recent vaping problem amongst the students. This prevented them from hiding in the bathroom and left them exposed in the hallway.

Parental Notification, Accountability, and Reunification

Once word about an incident, whether in a child-care center or in the neighborhood, is known in the community, the parents will attempt to get to the scene. Police are likely to close roads in the area, so parents are not going to be able to reach the facility. Ensuring you have a plan in place regarding how to communicate with parents during and after a disaster is important. As part of your general emergency-preparedness plan, you should have policies and procedures regarding how parents are to be notified and how you communicate with parents during an incident. Often, this is best done through text messaging or social media, as the volume of telephone calls can quickly overwhelm a child-care program.
Be sure you discuss your emergency-communication plan with parents in advance of any disaster so they are aware of the communication channels that you will be using.

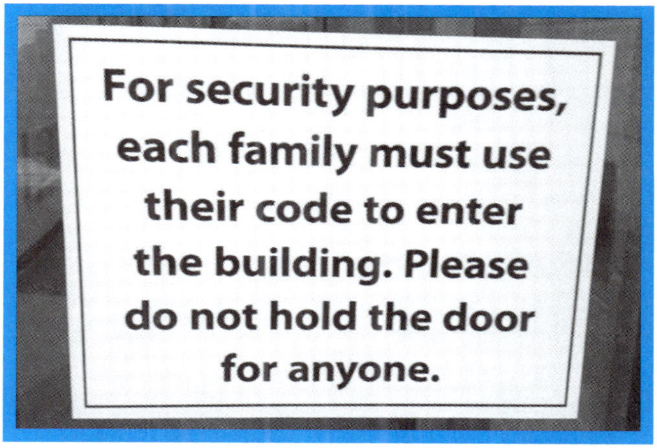

It is important to keep track of the individuals who are inside your program each day. This allows for accountability in the case of an emergency. Institute procedures that allow the front office and the individual classrooms to have accurate daily head counts. This will allow staff members to quickly determine who is missing and who is present during an emergency situation. First responders will be looking to the staff at the child-care program as a resource and will be reliant on the staff to help determine who is missing and who is accounted for. Given the importance of this task, it is recommended that you incorporate a head count or some exercise regarding accountability into your required emergency drills.

The reunification of parents and children is never easy, especially under the stress of an emergency or tragedy. Keep up-to-date emergency contact information and photographs of the children. Maintain a current list of parents and guardians who are authorized to pick up each child. This information should be updated regularly, at least quarterly, and the list should be stored in at least two locations. Many programs create a classroom-by-classroom list that is included inside the emergency-preparedness kit in each classroom. Ideally, one copy of this information should be on paper and another copy should be electronic. Given the wide availability of technology, consider emailing the list to yourself or storing it in a cloud-based storage system so that it is accessible if you are away from your facility or are unable to access your facility. In the event of an emergency, staff can use the list and photos to make sure that the children are reunited with their families when it is safe to do so.

4

Situational Awareness and Creating a Culture of Safety

Situational awareness refers to the ability to be aware of the space, surroundings, and things happening around you. In this chapter, we will discuss ways to become more situationally aware, recognize times when you can easily be distracted, and discuss tools to use to prevent or mitigate those distractions.

Not paying attention to your surroundings and getting distracted is easy to do. For instance, child-care professionals could be intently focused on a child's needs or on several children in a class without noticing other circumstances around them. Or a conversation with a parent could be engaging and in-depth, pulling focus away from the surroundings. It is simply a good reminder to understand how quickly dangerous situations can evolve and the need to be aware of cues that indicate changes in surroundings.

Situational awareness is important for a number of different reasons: protection, warning, and information recall. The sooner we can identify that something is out of place, the more time we are going to have to react. This affords us time to take action to protect ourselves, such as running away, locking doors, or grabbing an improvised weapon. It also allows us time to warn others by calling 911, making an emergency announcement, or pressing a panic alarm.

Quickly recognizing things that are out of the ordinary will help us in providing information to responding law enforcement officers. Details can be important: What color was the vehicle? What state were the license plates from? Which way did the person run? Law enforcement will use that information to apprehend a suspect.

While acting quickly when things are unusual or uncomfortable is our goal, it is not always easy. The body has built-in mechanisms that attempt to justify abnormalities to protect us from scary situations. Simply put, sometimes in stressful situations our minds attempt to excuse things so that we do not seem paranoid. We call these mechanisms *normalcy bias* and *social proof*. To better understand these concepts and how they can be applied, we will consider lessons learned from the Columbine school shooting.

From the time the first gunshots were fired at Columbine in 1999, there was a six- to eight-minute delay before the first 911 call. The reason for that delay was *normalcy bias*—people rationalized what was going on, unable to process that the noises could be gunshots, assuming or convincing themselves that perhaps the noise could be a car backfiring, fireworks, or a senior prank. The idea of hearing gunshots at a school in 1999 was highly unusual.

The other issue at play was *social proof*, the desire to avoid looking foolish in front of our friends, colleagues, or even strangers. So, again, people try to adhere to norms, even in times of an emergency. There have been other scenarios in which dozens of police officers respond to an emergency call, or sprinkler systems go off in a building, and people stand by or watch because they still think the event is a drill, when in fact all signs point toward a real emergency scenario. It's difficult to overcome these biases and quickly come to terms with reality as unexpected or hard-to-handle events unfold.

The sooner that we can recognize things that look out of place in our surroundings, the better. You know what goes on in your home and in your place of work every day. You know which people, cars, smells, sights, and sounds are familiar. If something out of the ordinary appears, we need to take notice. Not everything that looks out of place leads to a dangerous event; however, it's important to take stock of your environment and be prepared to react.

> **When I first heard a woman screaming, 'Active shooter!' while dashing down the office hallway, my first thought was that it must be a drill."**
>
> —Christi Dewar, survivor of the Virginia Beach Municipal Center shooting, June 2019

Another important part of overall situational awareness is being aware of the risks and threats to your program and knowing how to minimize them. We will discuss this in more detail as we examine how rings of security apply to early childhood settings.

For the past several years, there has been an effort to harden soft targets. If you have attended a professional sporting event recently, you have undoubtedly noticed a vast difference in the levels of security that are present. Many sporting events now ban bags or require the use of see-through backpacks, limit what items you can bring into the venue with you, and even subject you to a metal-detector screening prior to entry. These measures were implemented to harden potential terrorist targets and make it more difficult for bad actors to enter these venues undetected. While these measures will certainly not prevent every possible situation from occurring, they do act as a deterrent.

Often bad actors look for easy targets: the unlocked automobile, the person not paying attention to his surroundings, the building with the door that is left unlocked. In the spirit of keeping ourselves and the children entrusted in our care safe, we have to begin thinking about simple ways that we can harden our buildings and increase our security. Our challenge is two-fold—maintaining the nurturing and caring environment that is essential for the children and families, while also keeping the reality of budgetary constraints in mind. Throughout this chapter, we will explore strategies designed to increase security with these challenges in mind.

Rings of Security

Securing your facility goes hand-in-hand with increasing your situational awareness. Doing so creates a safer and more secure environment for your employees, the children, and their families. Identifying a problem as early as possible will provide you with additional time to react. Consider the White House, which is arguably one of the most secure buildings in the world. Just as the White House utilizes multiple rings of security to prevent a breach, you too should consider the rings of security surrounding your facility. At the White House, as at many other highly secured buildings, there are gates, checkpoints, doorways, and other barriers meant to screen those attempting to enter and to allow only permitted individuals to do so. Similar thinking and concepts can be applied to child-care programs and other environments.

As you think about your child-care program, consider how many doors, how many stopping points, how many checkpoints you would have to go through between the time you pulled up in your parking lot and the time you entered the same room as the children. All of those rings represent opportunities to stop bad things from happening. It's important to take stock of those systems you already have in place and to think about what else could be modified to improve the rings of security at your facility.

Outermost Ring of Security

For many child-care programs, the outermost ring of security is the outdoor environment that encompasses a facility's parking lot, outdoor play areas, and the surrounding neighborhood. Consider nearby local business, public spaces, and attractions that may affect operations. In particular, be mindful of transitional spaces, such as gas stations, pawn shops, convenience stores, banks, and other areas that allow for quick access into and out of an area. While everyday business and activities happen in transitional spaces, such locations also can be targeted for crime and bad behavior, given how easy it is to enter and leave the spaces.

Consider whether you have cameras in your facility. If not, you can still consider external visibility on the property. For many child-care programs, the parking lot is the first place where it will be evident that something out of the ordinary is occurring. Examples of "something out of the ordinary" could be a person loitering in the parking lot, a person taking more-than-usual interest in the children in the playground area, a person trying to peek into classrooms from the parking lot, a service vehicle (unmarked or from a company that was not called), or a vehicle parked in the lot overnight or during off-peak hours. These are simply examples, but it's important to pay attention to your surroundings and notice when there's a change in your environment that could have the potential to be a threat. The sooner something out of place can be identified, the better.

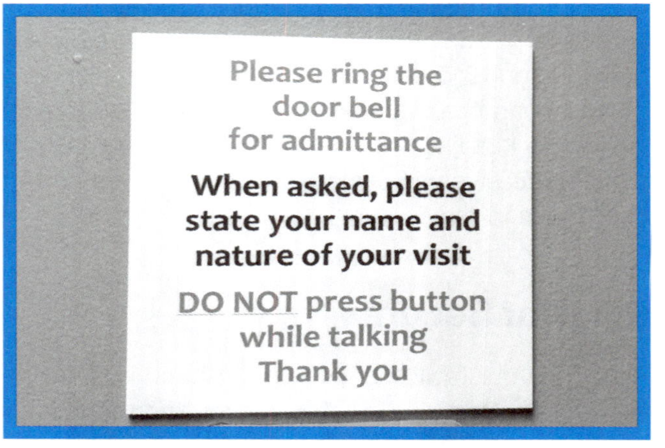

Also, be mindful of other establishments near your facility that can cause increased pedestrian and vehicular traffic, such as schools, libraries, places of worship, recreation facilities, shopping areas, and so on. When you are in a high-traffic area, it is helpful to stagger outdoor time and activities to avoid peak hours. For instance, if your child-care center is in a strip mall that has businesses and restaurants, then lunchtime from 11:30 a.m. to 1:30 p.m. may be a busy time, with many people passing by the playground area. If so, the children's outdoor time could be scheduled from 10:00 a.m. to 11:00 a.m. and again from 2:00 p.m. to 3:30 p.m. to avoid peak lunch hours. The goal is to be a bit unpredictable and not have easily recognizable routines that can be exploited by bad actors. By modifying our schedules, we can reduce the number of unknown individuals in the area when children are outside, making it easier to spot potential threats, such as people lingering or who appear to be out of place.

To evaluate your outermost ring of security, walk around your building and take notes on areas for improvement. Specifically look at lighting, obstructions to sight lines, places where people could hide and ambush an unwitting person, places where people could scale fencing and other barriers, and overgrowth in surrounding landscaping.

Identify areas that are dimly lit, and work to install or replace lighting. This is particularly important in the winter and fall, as staff members will be approaching and departing work in the dark. Garbage-disposal and dumpster areas are usually areas of concern because they offer a place where individuals can hide, and these areas are often dimly lit. Somebody can easily climb on top of a dumpster

and hop right over a fence and into your secured area. People can hide behind dumpsters and use them for an ambush. Dumpsters near buildings are probably for convenience because people don't want to walk very far carrying the garbage, but pushing a dumpster farther away from the building would be safer. Where possible, encourage staff members to park away from these areas.

Take other steps to secure your outermost ring, such as increasing your visibility by ensuring trees, bushes, and hedges are trimmed. For staff members who park in areas with dim lighting, implement a system whereby they can move their cars closer to the building before they leave at night. Also, organize a system through which staff members walk out together so that no one is alone. Where possible, park large vehicles, such as vans and buses, away from the front doors; avoid blocking visibility out of the windows so that you can more easily evaluate threats before they arrive.

Our goal is to create the biggest outermost ring. That way, we can detect problems in advance, before they show up at our front door or inside our programs. After evaluating your external environment, make a list of potential areas of concern and possible solutions to mitigate the threats. Prioritize the list, and start taking action to improve your outermost ring of security.

Middle Ring of Security

The middle ring is the area immediately before the entry of your child-care facility. Typically, the middle ring of security is a physical barrier of entry, such as a set of double doors, a residential front door, or a check-in area. The middle ring of security should be secured at all times, even during pickup and drop-off hours. Front doors or entryways should never be unlocked or propped open.

You will need to make important decisions regarding the middle ring of security. Specifically, child-care programs need to develop and implement policies regarding who can enter your facility. It is vital that you enforce these policies consistently to hold staff and visitors accountable every day. Just as child-care programs check children in and out each day, you will need to develop similar processes for visitors. A well-designed, secure child-care program will deny entry to anyone who has not been properly screened; therefore, you must establish appropriate policies in advance to prevent the entry of unauthorized individuals.

For centers, this level of security includes having a policy in place for prospective parents who want to tour the facility. And again, it's 100 percent okay for you to tell somebody no. If someone comes up, knocks on the door, and says, "Hey, I'd like a tour," you are well within your rights to just respond, "We're really happy that you're here, and we're glad you're showing an interest in our program. I'm sorry, but we do not offer unscheduled tours. Please call our office, and we can set something up." Visitors should be asked to fill out a form with their basic personal information (name, address, contact information) as well as the make, model, and license-plate number of their vehicle and a copy of their driver's license. This process gets back to situational awareness and information recall. Having this information may be important in the future, especially if you continue to see the person or vehicle in the area after the tour has concluded.

Visitors who fail to provide this information should be denied a tour, especially when children are present. Be alert to cues that something may be out of place. For instance, if the driver's license or license plate does not match the city and state where you are located, then simply say, "I see you are not from the area. What brings you here today?" Such a simple question allows you to gain more information and mitigate threats, while doing so in a nonconfrontational manner.

For family/home child-care providers, be cognizant of individuals who may attempt to gain access to your home throughout the day. For mail and package delivery, establish a system whereby packages are left outside your door rather than having someone opening the door to directly engage with the delivery person. Recently, some delivery companies have started subcontracting with other entities to support the final delivery of packages. This could mean that people dropping off packages are driving a regular car or an unmarked van and do not have a uniform. In these instances, it is even more difficult to know whether the person approaching your front door should be doing so.

When service or maintenance, such as that provided by electricians, plumbers, or repair workers, is required at the facility, ensure you have information about who will be performing these services. Will the workers be driving a company vehicle? Will they wear uniforms? Will they have company identification? If an individual shows up and you are not satisfied that he is from the company, call the company and have them verify the individual's identity as their employee. These are helpful tips that any homeowner can and should take to stay safe; however, these steps are even more critical with children on-site.

Any time the door is opened, an outside threat has the potential to enter your space. Now, of course, most people will not be a threat; however, the purpose of having secure systems and locked doors is to appropriately screen and allow entry only for those who need to be on-site with children. The sturdiest doors and most expensive security systems are useless if the door is propped open all day—or if the combination code to the door is 123# and hasn't been changed in five years. Similarly, if an intercom system is in place, the technology needs to work, and the staff using it need to feel empowered to refuse entry when appropriate or to ask for additional information regarding the nature of a visit. You should change locks and codes to security systems if or when a staff member is fired or a parent or visitor is visibly upset or no longer allowed entry.

Post signs to inform visitors of who may enter and how to go about requesting access. Signs let the visitors know what your expectations are and where they should be going. Also, if you see someone trying to get in at a door where a sign is posted, you will be alerted to a possible problem: "Wow, that person is not supposed to be there. There's a sign that says that, and she's still trying to get in."

Inform staff and families that *tailgating* (when an unauthorized person slips in through a door before it closes) and *piggybacking* (when an authorized person allows someone to follow him through a door to a secure area) are not allowed. Unfortunately, many times well-meaning parents allow and encourage piggybacking by holding the door open for the individuals behind them. While we recognize that most parents do this because they want to be friendly, there are potential safety ramifications of these actions. Through piggybacking, well-meaning parents may inadvertently provide access to former staff members, parents who have recently lost custody of their children, or even strangers unaffiliated with the facility. At Virginia Tech, the shooter was supposed to have no access to the building. However, he successfully made entry due to security failures. Students allowed the shooter to piggyback through the locked door. It is of paramount importance that doors be locked and secured throughout the workday. Although inconvenient, this practice also includes busy times, such as pickup and drop-off.

WORKING WITH PARENTS TO MAINTAIN SAFETY

- **The safety of your child is our number-one priority.**
- **You are an important part of our team.**
- **Be sure the door closes behind you when entering and exiting the building.**
- **Do not hold doors open for other families or individuals.**
- **If you encounter a visitor, please ask if you can assist and direct the person to the front desk.**
- **Update your contact information on a regular basis.**
- **Regularly update who is approved to pick up your child as well.**
- **If you see something out of the ordinary, please say something. Remember, safety is everyone's responsibility.**

Inner Ring of Security

The inner ring of security focuses on personnel, policies, and physical barriers on the inside of your program. Think about your program. When an individual is inside your program's front door, how many doors, barriers, and obstacles does he have to get through or overcome before he can physically make contact with a child? These components of the inner ring of security represent potential areas to either slow or stop an intruder. However, for these measures to work most efficiently, child-care programs need to ensure policies are in place and followed consistently. For example, if doors are to remain closed during operating hours, then wedges or other items should not be used to prop them open.

Further, the consistent application of your identification policies is very important. Staff should never feel uncomfortable asking a stranger for identification and his purpose within the program space. Remember, the inner ring should ideally be populated only by verified and trusted individuals. In many ways, the inner ring is our last line of defense against bad or violent actions.

Creating a Culture of Safety

A culture of safety means that everyone within a child-care program community must take responsibility to make the space safer. Part of developing this culture means casting a more critical eye toward those approaching the space and ensuring they are vetted before allowing entry. Being kind and welcoming is always recommended; however, as part of the culture of safety, it is okay to question someone and say no. Doing so may feel confrontational at first. Make sure parents and staff know about the new policies and safety measures so they know the importance of everyone doing their part to keep the space safe for the children. Child-care programs have an even greater responsibility for safety than other businesses, as they are entrusted with our community's youngest individuals.

Work with parents to proactively create a culture of safety, one in which it is okay to question those individuals who are seeking to gain entry into your program. Empower staff and parents with the tools they need to help maintain your facility as a safe space for their children. By engaging families in this process, we also gain additional sets of eyes that can be on the lookout for things out of the ordinary and for potential problems.

Parents need to know that holding doors open for others, propping doors open, and not following safety policies puts everyone at risk. All these changes can and should be shared kindly, while still emphasizing the importance of safety. Explain the reasons for changes in the program and how they will improve safety for the children. The culture of safety means that not everyone can enter the space if or when they want to; instead, the staff is empowered to uphold the policies and actions that keep the children safe.

Identification within a child-care program is recommended. Requiring employees to wear identification would help first responders in the immediate aftermath of an incident. For registration of children and families, it is a good practice to get a photo of parents and children in preparation for an emergency situation. These photos could be used for family reunification purposes after an emergency. They could also be used to deny people access to the facility, if necessary. If an individual is a known or potential threat to the people in a child-care program—perhaps a parent who has lost custody of a child, a recently fired employee, or an individual who has a restraining order against him—photos of the individual should be available to all staff to make them aware.

Ensure That All Staff Are Trained

Child-care programs occasionally will have substitutes or temporary staff at the facility. It is important to ensure that staff members are brought up to speed on the program's policies and procedures for safety. All employees, both permanent and temporary, need to know what to do in an emergency and feel empowered to respond appropriately.

Substitute teachers were at the school on the day of the shooting at Marjory Stoneman Douglas High School. In that instance, the high school students could educate the substitutes on the proper procedures. However, in a child-care setting, the children are too young to educate temporary staff on policies and procedures for emergencies. This training also includes ensuring substitute staff have all necessary keys, lock combinations, intercom and telephone codes, and so on. So, take the necessary steps to inform and educate substitutes and temporary staff on emergency-preparedness policies and procedures before these staff members begin work.

Training is important to enable personnel to react appropriately if confronted with an active-shooter situation. If you are in harm's way, decide rapidly on the safest course of action based on the scenario that is unfolding. Because these situations evolve quickly, fast decisions could mean the difference between life and death.

The reality is that first responders and police are minutes away when called for help, but often the first few seconds of an event are critical. Your emergency number, such as 911 or the number used in your country, must be called as soon as possible. Programs also need to prepare to be on their own for a few minutes and need to practice how they will respond. Staff members need to be trained to be calm in emergencies and to utilize the skills they have practiced. Projecting calm and confidence will help children stay calm in a crisis, too. The tools and techniques you use to keep children calm every day can be translated for emergency response and put to use as well. For instance, using a light-up glow ball to draw their attention, telling them that you're playing the quiet game, providing them with coloring books, or giving them hard candy to suck on could keep them calm. Telling them that everything is going to be okay but it's extremely important that they are very quiet can be helpful, too.

Internal Communication

Planning efforts should be flexible and take into consideration the unexpected. For instance, an event could happen when children and staff are outside of their classroom, perhaps in a hallway, or backyard or on the playground. Think through various scenarios and how information could be shared across staff in a facility at the time of an incident. Depending on the situation, either staying in one location or moving elsewhere could be the safer option, and being able to communicate internally with others who may have more information about the scenario is important.

All staff should be instructed and empowered to make an announcement if there is an intruder on the premises. Such incidents do not always start at the front desk, so all staff should to be prepared to alert others if they see something. For instance, if there's a custody issue and someone is trying to target a single child, the intruder may attempt to bypass the front desk and go directly to that child's classroom through other entrances. This can become an issue in programs that allow parents to go directly to the classrooms for pickup and drop-off. For those programs that have classrooms with external doors, intruders could attempt entry from the playground or side of the building instead of the front door. That is why it is of paramount importance to ensure that all exterior doors are locked during business hours and not propped open. Visitors should come through one point of entry: the front door.

For staff to communicate across rooms, an intercom, cell phones, or even walkie-talkies could work. It is important to test the technology, ensuring that it functions properly and that all staff members know how to use it. If walkie-talkies are used, then get in the habit of using them every day. Some child-care programs use their walkie-talkies to make morning announcements or read religious passages at the start of each day. They rotate which classroom makes the announcement, so that every teacher gains experience with the walkie-talkies and so that all staff have their walkie-talkies on and regularly practice their use.

Regardless of the chosen system, a backup system should be identified and tested, too. A simple backup could be something as simple as an air horn. An air horn placed in every classroom could be an appropriate tool to notify others of a dangerous situation unfolding. In addition to an internal communication system, staff should have each other's cell phone numbers saved in their own phones in advance of an emergency. If staff become separated in an emergency, having their colleagues' numbers stored will allow them to communicate. These should be updated regularly as new staff come on board and existing cell phone numbers change. As previously mentioned, some child-care programs will use an intercom system for internal communication. There are a few things you should know about intercom systems if you have one or are thinking about purchasing one. Intercoms are now relatively inexpensive and can be a feature within a phone system. The biggest issue with intercoms is staff not being trained on how to use the technology or empowered to use it for emergency response. It is imperative that all staff know how to use the intercom system and that it's tested to ensure all rooms can hear the intercom and respond with an intercom message as well. When testing intercoms, the volume should be noted and adjusted to be sure those throughout the space can hear it.

Be aware that many intercom systems work both inside and outside of facilities. So if you are conducting a drill, it is always important to lead with, "This is a drill," to avoid inadvertently creating confusion. Make sure to speak clearly and to ensure that what you are saying cannot be misunderstood. Code words, such as "code red," often create greater confusion, as not everyone will know or remember what they mean. A simple announcement could be, "This is a drill. There is an active shooter in the building. There is an active shooter in the building." Of course, in an actual event, you would drop "this is a drill" and instead say, "There is an active shooter in the building. There is an active shooter in the building."

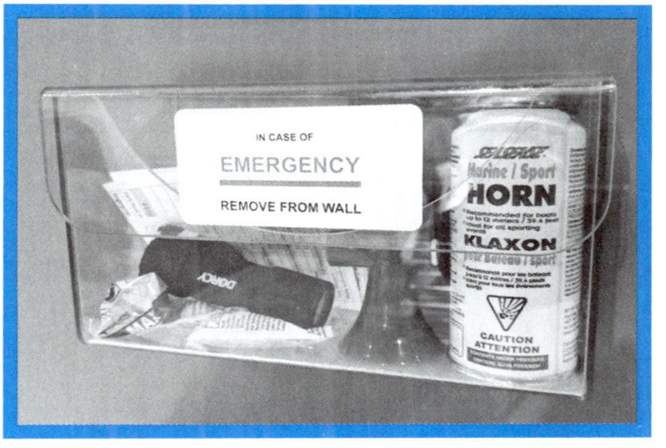

Repeating the important information a couple of times is a good practice. First, test these systems without children in the rooms. Then, with children present, test again; the volume will need to be louder. The same type of drills and practice can be applied to other technology systems beyond intercoms, such as walkie-talkies.

Although facility-wide code words are not recommended during an active-shooter situation, there may be times when a code word is helpful. Code words are useful when a situation has the potential to become dangerous, but the danger has not yet occurred. These code words would be used to communicate discreetly among staff members to indicate something is out of place, someone feels uncomfortable, or someone is in danger. For example, a code word could be used to deescalate a situation and buy time for others to call for help. The keys, of course, will be to have a set code word or term, make sure the staff know what that code word is and what it means, and practice using it before a real emergency occurs.

Consider a parent who has lost custody of his child. He shows up at your program and wants to pick up his child. To buy some time, the person at the front desk could feign compliance and tell the parent that he is going to call back to the classroom to have the child brought to the front entrance. There are many legitimate reasons for doing so, such as not disturbing the other children during nap time or an activity, so the parent should not be alarmed by this. The worker at the front desk would then make a call and indicate that the parent is at the front of the building and is requesting his child. Prior to hanging up, the person at the front desk would also insert the code word or term into the conversation: "Oh, and the bakery called and wanted me to remind you to pick up your blueberry muffins on the way home tonight." There are no blueberry muffins, but the saying sounds completely innocuous; therefore, it will not tip off the parent. The parent thinks you are complying and that he is getting what he wants. In reality, with the code word, you have just alerted another staff member that you are in trouble and need assistance. Now, out of sight of the parent, the other staff member can call 911 and begin taking action to protect the children and staff.

Reporting Incidents

Beyond internal communication, reporting incidents is also an extremely important step. Staff should know the policies on reporting and should feel empowered to report suspicious behavior when they see it. Developing a culture of reporting incidents is important for any child-care program. We will explore reporting possible emergencies in the next chapter.

5 Taking Action

One of the easiest ways to deal with a potentially dangerous situation is to remove yourself from the situation or environment from the start. For instance, if you're walking down the street and see someone who seems out of place, the easiest response you can take is to cross the street and distance yourself from that person. Similarly, if you're taking children out to the playground but see someone suspicious sitting in the nearby parking lot, then change your routine and keep the children inside for the time being. The police can deal with various situations that seem threatening on your property; you do not need to investigate the situation yourself or put yourself in harm's way.

Run, Fight, Hide

Unfortunately, there will be times when we just don't notice a threat—it happens too fast, and all of a sudden the danger is upon us. We will have to take some action in the form of running, hiding, or fighting. The U.S. Department of Homeland Security adapted the mantra, "Run, Hide, Fight," as a way to help people recall steps that can be taken during an active-shooter incident. These steps are designed for adults and older children in schools and child-care programs. In the case of infants and very young children, hiding is typically the best option. We will explore each of these techniques in greater detail below so providers can understand their options in the event of an active-shooter scenario.

Active-shooter situations can change rapidly. Therefore, responses to them must be flexible and contain a wide array of options. As these situations evolve, options need to be reviewed and re-evaluated to determine the best course of action. For example, in the initial stages of an active-shooter incident, the best response may be to hide. However, after a few minutes, if the situation changes, then running may become the more appropriate option. The point here is that active-shooter responses can vary and are not easily scripted. Our options of "run, fight, or hide" are not sequential and may be used at various times during an active-shooter situation. We can use these techniques as the situation warrants during our response. (The Santa Ana, California, School Police have posted a video on

YouTube.com called "SAUSD Run Hide Fight (Elementary School)." This video demonstrates each of these responses.)

No single technique is the best; instead, child-care programs need to be equipped with multiple options so staff can make their best judgment call as a situation unfolds. These events are unpredictable, and active shooters are always changing their techniques to try to harm as many people as possible. Have a wide variety of options and train on those options. A well-prepared child-care program is one with staff who feel empowered, have the necessary knowledge and skills, have practiced and drilled for various scenarios, and can stay calm and make decisions quickly during stressful times.

Run

If safe to do so, running and escaping from the immediate area of danger is the best option. Depending on the age of the children in your program, running may be a viable option. The term *run* means doing so with a purpose, escaping from the immediate danger zone, and getting far away from the incident. Generally, most adults, young children, and older children are able to run.

In advance of a scenario, create a plan on how and where to run, in case that option should be warranted. For instance, if a classroom has only one door and that door faces danger, running may mean throwing a chair through a window to create a new exit. Staff need to feel comfortable and empowered that making decisions like this during an active-shooter event is okay and warranted. They will not get in trouble; in fact, they will be lauded for taking steps to keep themselves and the children they care for safe.

Consider escape routes from classrooms, hallways, entry areas, playgrounds, parking lots, and other spaces. Consider how many doors you pass before you exit the building from your classroom, and of these doors, how many could you open and how many are locked? Identify these exit routes ahead of time just in case the situation changes and you find yourself in an unexpected location when an actual scenario is unfolding.

If the running technique is used, get low, use objects to conceal the escape, and run in the direction of safety. Fire drills offer an opportunity to think about where to run, but it is likely that the reunification point used for fire drills is not far enough. Survey the area around your child-care program and identify locations to which staff and children could run. Such locations may include a nearby shopping center, a grocery store, a family residence, a restaurant—any place that would provide some refuge indoors. Some child-care programs have formalized these relationships by entering agreements with nearby businesses that allow them access to the space during an emergency. In some cases, the partnering businesses even provide keys and/or door combinations for quick access in an emergency.

Early childhood providers often find themselves outdoors with children, whether on the playground or elsewhere. Generally, being outside provides more options for running than being inside, as there are multiple exits, not just doors and windows. The barrier that child-care programs may face outdoors is a fence, which can present its own set of challenges. As part of preparedness efforts, child-care programs should review and consider the gates enclosing playgrounds and other areas. Gates should not be permanently locked, and if there's a key or a combination lock, all staff should be able to open it. Be sure that all staff know how to operate the gate and the gate latch. Further, gates should not be rusted shut or be obstructed by dirt, leaves, or other debris that prevent them from being opened. Special care should be taken in winter when snow and ice can impair gate functions. Maintain gates to ensure that they can open freely.

Exiting from a playground must be practiced in drills. Even when staff say they know how to operate gates, in practice they occasionally struggle to do so quickly. While this may seem extremely simple, it's better to practice simple things like this in advance of a scenario than to struggle with a gate when danger is imminent.

In addition to examining the gates, also consider the height of fences surrounding a child-care program. Consider whether staff have the physical strength to lift children up and over the fence. Also, check the bottom of the fence. Sometimes, the bottom portion of a fence is not attached in a very secure manner, and you may be able to lift up or pull back the bottom and scoot children under the fence.

OUTSIDE ESCAPE ROUTES

- Identify doors, gates, and other exit routes.
- Identify a destination where you can run for safety.
- Ensure that any doors or gates are functional.
- Ensure that staff have keys or combinations if gates are locked and know how to open the gates quickly.
- Identify equipment or landscaping you could use for concealment as you run.

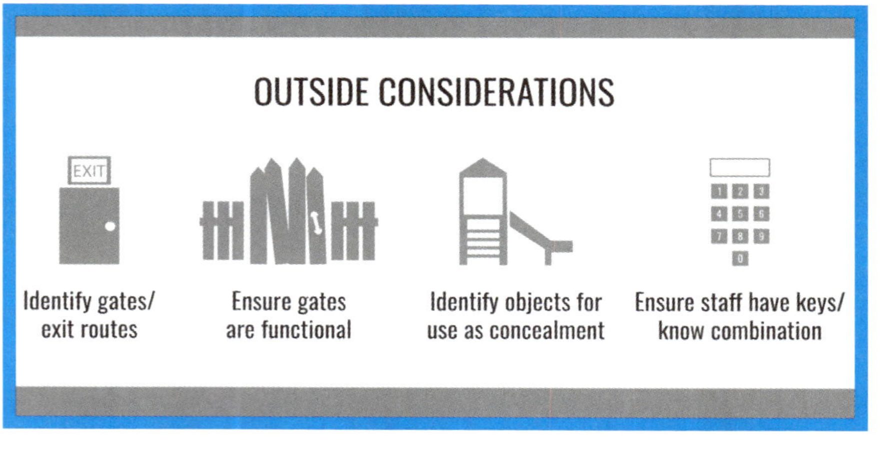

Hide

In the context of active-shooter scenarios, the term *hide* does not mean get under the desk and wait as you would for an earthquake to pass. There are a few different aspects to consider. First, the strategy is to make sure the doors are locked and barricaded, the windows are covered, the lights are off, and the room looks completely unoccupied. Because an active shooter knows that time for an attack is limited, and because the goal is to do the most damage to the most people in the shortest amount of time, the shooter likely will pass up a room that looks vacant. So it is imperative to lock doors, place objects against them to make it difficult or impossible to open them from the outside, turn off lights, get in a safe position that is out of sight, and be quiet. Hiding can be a very effective option when executed properly.

If more than one staff member is in a given room, splitting up duties works best. For instance, one staff member can focus on turning off lights, blocking or covering windows, and locking and barricading doors. The second staff member can quietly move the children to safety.

Covering Your Windows

The goal is to make your room look unoccupied. This can be accomplished by covering the windows and turning out the lights. Windows can be covered in cost-effective ways. Programs often use cut-to-fit construction paper or fabric to quickly cover the windows. Once the covering is cut to size, Velcro strips or magnets are attached, allowing the covering to quickly adhere to the window frame without struggling with tape or other adhesive materials. Some programs even use these coverings to darken rooms for nap time. These coverings can easily be made in-house for little money. See these short videos for easy and inexpensive ways to cover windows: https://www.youtube.com/watch?v=1HslKyCIsGM and https://www.youtube.com/watch?v=Ip68PGRy-bg0

Preparing Hard Corners

Identify hard corners that will provide places to hide. Hard corners should be identified in advance as part of emergency response planning. The term *hard corner* means an area of a room that is difficult or impossible to see from the entry to the room. Using hard corners can be very effective. The theory behind a hard corner is that even if your lock and barricade fail and the intruder is able to look into the room, it will still appear unoccupied because no one will be in sight.

At Marjory Stoneman Douglas High School, students tried to hide in hard corners but could not do so effectively because the school had used those spaces for storage. Extra boxes and unused items were piled there, essentially making the hard corners useless for those seeking refuge. For hard corners to be effective, they must be kept free of such objects. Regular and routine practice will ensure that these locations are kept free from obstacles. Check the hard corners in your facility and clear out any debris. Make sure there is adequate room for adults and children to hide. Practicing and using hard corners during drills will help you assess whether they can appropriately be used as hiding locations.

When hiding with children in hard corners, child-friendly tools, such as a sound-free glow ball (a small ball that lights up when you hit it) and other silent toys, could be used to keep their attention and keep them quiet. Such items could be kept in an emergency backpack or kit or stowed in the hard corner. For instance, if bathrooms and closets will be used as hard corners, it's recommended to keep a glow ball or two in those locations. Child-care programs should feel free to practice techniques to keep children quiet and build upon other existing efforts that might exist outside of emergency preparedness. For example, distractions, such as hard-candy suckers, books, or lotion to keep their hands moving and senses alert, could occupy their attention and help them stay quiet. Such efforts should not be done daily, but do practice them so children know how to act when it's time to be very quiet.

Barricading Doors

Note that locking doors, by itself, is not a good enough solution because a lock can be shot out. Consider the classroom layout, including the locations of bookshelves, chairs, tables, cabinets, and coatracks that you could use to barricade a door. As you practice barricading doors, consider what pieces of furniture could be moved or rearranged to provide for a more efficient response. For example, if you are planning to use a particular bookcase as your barricade, then consider moving that bookcase close to the door. Sometimes, this can be as simple as changing the orientation of the classroom tables. This will save time during an actual emergency.

Just as there is not one typical building layout for early childhood facilities, there is not one standard design for the operation of doors. Inward-swinging doors open toward the classroom. Outward-swinging doors open away from the classroom into the hallway. Both types of doors can be effectively barricaded. Child-care programs should practice barricading both types, as an incident could happen in different rooms or locations. With either type, it is recommended to install locks that can be accessed from inside the classrooms. Many state fire marshal offices throughout the United States are currently revising or issuing variances for existing fire codes to allow for the installation and use of locking devices and mechanisms during active-shooter situations.

Inward-swinging doors can be effectively barricaded in a variety of ways. The key to barricading this type of door is to stack objects against the door to prevent it from opening. One of the most effective ways to barricade an inward-swinging door is to build a barricade that starts at the door itself and ends at an immovable object, such as a wall, support beam, or cabinetry that is secured to the floor. This prevents the door from opening because the door physically cannot move against the immovable object. For infant rooms, using cribs can be very effective. Simply line up the cribs from the door to a wall to create a barrier. Using cribs can be easy because they are on wheels, and often this type of barricade can be completed by one person, freeing up the others in the room to work with the infants.Place the cribs flat against the door and avoid the doorknob, as that can create a gap and in some cases can even damage the crib itself. The door should make contact with as much of the barricade item as possible. Avoid using door wedges that are included in wooden play sets or blocks because they are often sanded down and coated with a sealer that makes them very smooth and slippery. These wedges can slide across the floor with little force, making them less than ideal as barricades.

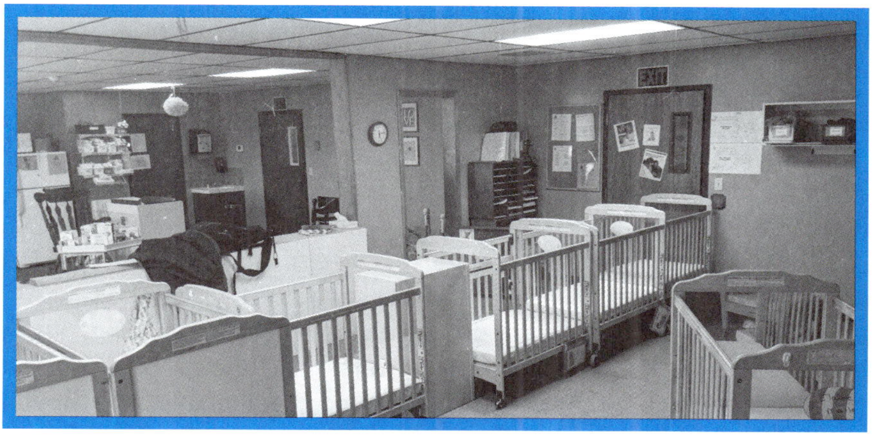

While some people think outward-swinging doors cannot be barricaded, this is not true. With practice, you can barricade an outward-swinging door just as effectively and quickly as an inward-swinging door. Doors that swing out into the hallway are common in public schools to allow a quick exit from the classroom in case of emergency. Indeed, this type of door is required by fire codes in some places so that the door can open freely and not get blocked by people attempting to exit.

The strategy for an outward-swinging door is to find items that are too big to fit through the doorway. Have you ever tried to put a piece of furniture through a doorway, but it was too big and got stuck? That is the concept that should be applied to outward-swinging doors. First, push these items up against the door to make a secure barrier. From there, wrap a rope or wire around the barrier furniture and attach it to the door. The exact method you use to attach it to the door will vary with the type of hardware that is installed on the door.

In the United States, the Americans with Disabilities Act (ADA) mandates that new facilities be accessible for people with physical disabilities. In the case of doors, they must open with a handicap-accessible switch, with a motion-operated mechanism, or with a handle that is easy for a person with a disability to reach and manipulate. To barricade doors with the ADA-approved door handles, the process is very simple: Attach the rope or wire to the handle and then loop it around the barrier. Because these handles are easy for children to grab and open, they are less common in the early childhood setting. Knobs can be used in a similar fashion but will require advance preparation and testing to ensure the rope or wire can be secured tightly enough around the knob. Another option is to install a simple eye hook on the door. This hook can then be used as a secure point to which you can attach a wire or rope.

In addition to building a barrier, some child-care programs expand upon the eye-hook concept. Install two eye hooks—one in the door and one in the nearby wall. They must be anchored into a stud or drilled into concrete to ensure they are stable and solid. If they are secured by small screws or into drywall, the eye hooks will fail with little pressure.

Next, cut a high-quality piece of wire and install a hook on each end. To secure the door, one hook goes onto the eye hook in the door and the other onto the eye hook in the wall. Once installed in this manner, the wire prevents the door from opening. Some fire codes allow for this type of mechanism (since it is not a permanently fixed device), but some do not. Check your local fire codes to determine whether or not you can use this device.

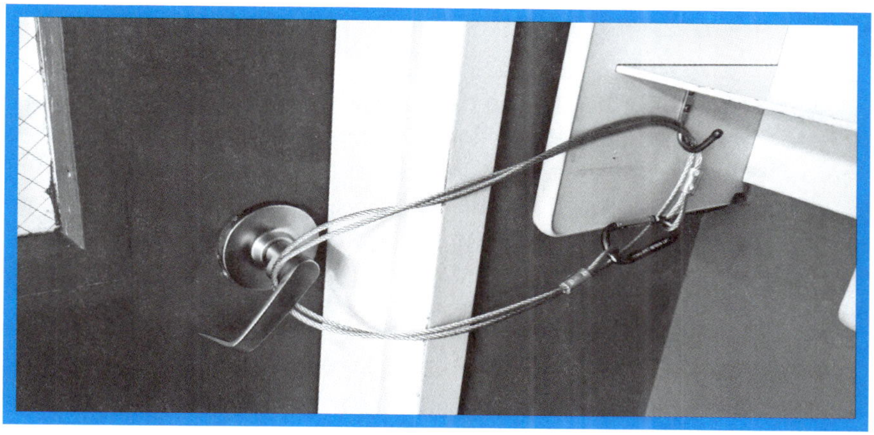

If you look closely, you can see that a rope is tied to one of the hooks in a cubby. The other end of the rope is tied to the door handle (not visible in this photo).

Fight

If you find yourself face to face with a dangerous person and with no opportunity to run or hide, then it is important to fight. Fighting could really be described as surviving—protecting yourself and the children against someone who is trying to hurt you. At this point, all options are on the table. Remember, having an active shooter on the property is not the experience of your typical day. Child-care programs need to empower their staff and teach them that everyone has permission to do whatever it takes to protect themselves and the children.

In the report "Active Shooter Incidents in the United States in 2016 and 2017" about the fifty active-shooter incidents in those two years, the FBI found that in ten incidents, citizens confronted the shooter. In 80 percent of those incidents in which citizens confronted the shooter, one or more citizens safely and successfully acted to end the shooting.

Another example of bystander involvement is from Israel. In 103 suicide attacks from 2000 to 2003, bystanders became involved in forty. A. J. Heightman, editor in chief of the *Journal of Emergency Medical Services*, reported in "Safety Considerations at Active Shooter and Mass Casualty Events," his address to the 2019 National Emergency Medical Services Safety Summit, that bystander involvement resulted in an approximately 70 percent reduction in the overall number of fatalities as compared to events with no bystander involvement. These numbers are incredibly powerful and underscore the importance of fighting as an effective response tool.

When you decide to fight, it is important to act extremely quickly and use the resources around you. Your action could be as simple as hitting a shooter over the head with a vacuum cleaner or broom or even throwing an object toward the shooter to distract and startle him. In fact, according to a report by ABC News, during a 2018 shooting at a yoga studio in Tallahassee, Florida, when the shooter paused for a brief moment, a man in the yoga class rushed the shooter and hit him with a vacuum cleaner. The shooter fought back, hitting the man with his pistol. Instead of giving up, the heroic man went back after the shooter, this time with a broom. He survived. Ultimately, the shooter was killed by a self-inflicted gunshot wound before police arrived.

Prior to the confrontation, two people were shot and killed, but the man in the yoga class who confronted the shooter prevented additional bystanders from dying and effectively ended the shooting. Almost all active shooters plan for their attack, yet they rarely plan for their escape. Any distractions, obstacles, or harm to them could slow them down or stop them entirely.

In a 2018 active-shooter incident in Noblesville, Indiana, according to the *IndyStar*, a thirteen-year-old walked into a middle-school science class where students were taking an exam. The FBI reported that the shooter in this incident was the youngest shooter among all incidents in 2018. The shooter injured one student with several bullets, and then the science teacher threw a small basketball at the shooter, tackled him, and ultimately disarmed him. The science teacher was shot three times, but he lived to share his story. The teacher said that he handled the shooting so well because he had undergone a training course in advance of the shooting. He said, "I had mentally prepared what would happen in my room if a shooting were to happen there. I had thought about it before."

According to a report by Nicole Chavez of CNN, a rural school district in Pennsylvania put buckets of rocks in each classroom to arm students with a self-defense tool in the event of an active-shooter scenario. Some child-care programs have also taken steps to do the same and have even painted the rocks as art. Small rocks could disorient and perhaps distract an active shooter so that more forceful action could be taken.

Reporting the Emergency

When seconds matter, help is minutes away. Reporting an emergency as soon as possible allows law enforcement to arrive on the scene faster. There are some special considerations to take into account when reporting an emergency.

Fire Alarm

Fire alarms are for alerting people to fires and should not be used to report an active-shooter emergency. The alarm may be local only and not transmitted to a dispatch center. If the alarm is transmitted to a dispatch center, often the fire department does not respond with the police department. Further, firefighters are unarmed and are not equipped to provide much assistance against a gun-wielding attacker. Fire alarms are loud and can add to the confusion, making it difficult to detect where the shooting is coming from. During a fire alarm, people are trained to leave the safety of the classroom and go into the hallway. Pulling the fire alarm may unnecessarily put your colleagues and the children in danger.

Active shooters look for target-rich environments. Most people are trained to exit a building when the fire alarm sounds. During the shooting at Marjory Stoneman Douglas High School, the fire alarm was activated, causing students to crowd into the third-floor hallway. Unbeknownst to them, the shooter was actively searching for targets on the second floor. Luckily, the majority of students on the third floor were able to escape to safety before the shooter arrived on that floor. When responding to a fire alarm, be extra aware of your surroundings and be ready to quickly retreat to safety. Fire alarms should be approached with an extra sense of caution to be sure it is a legitimate sounding of the alarm and not an attempted ambush.

Panic Buttons and Burglar Alarms

Systems such as panic buttons or burglar alarms can be effective as long as they are properly monitored. Most of these systems are monitored by a central dispatch system. The dispatch system may be in your town, in another state, or even in another country. When an alarm is received, the dispatch station will typically attempt to make contact with an individual, such as an owner or director, to verify that the alarm is legitimate. They often do this before calling law enforcement, as many municipalities have instituted fines for false alarms. While such verification may be effective in avoiding fines for false alarms, it is certainly not effective in the event of an active-shooter incident.

As the monitoring center is busy calling individuals, time is ticking by. Therefore, any child-care center that may plan to rely on a panic button or burglar alarm system as its primary means of alerting law enforcement must have an understanding of how the incoming alarm will be handled by the dispatch center. The leading practice is to have push-button panic alarms immediately go to the local law enforcement agency. Motion detection and window alarms (especially after hours when the building is vacant) will trigger the alarm company to attempt to make contact with the individuals on the call list before notifying the police.

Calling 911

The most effective way to report an emergency to the authorities is to call 911 (or the emergency number for your country). Child-care center leadership should have conversations with staff on their first day regarding emergency procedures, especially dialing 911 in case of an emergency. For violence and active-shooter incidents, the leading practice is to empower all staff to call 911 in these situations. Also, directors should be sure to discuss any codes or procedures they would need to follow when calling 911. In some cases, internal phone systems require the user to dial a number or a code in order to reach an outside telephone line.

Make sure that all employees and parents and family members—anyone who is a part of your program—know the child-care program's physical address. Just as children are taught to learn their names, the names of their parents, and their addresses, adults need to know the street address of the child-care program in case of an emergency.

Calling 911 from a landline is the quickest way to ensure information is transmitted in a timely manner. Thanks to enhanced 911 in the United States, emergency dispatch centers automatically receive information about the name, location, police beat, and nearest fire and EMS units when a 911 landline call is received. Even if the caller is unable to speak, this information will still be transmitted.

Cell phone technology is constantly changing. The technology at emergency dispatch centers has struggled to keep up with the ever-changing landscape of mobile and cellular technology. Nowadays, it is common for cell phones to be jam-packed with the latest features and functions. Thanks to GPS, people can now order dinner, an Uber or Lyft ride to a specific location, and much more. However, even though this technology has advanced greatly, these advances have not translated over to 911 calls. There is no guarantee that dispatch will know a caller's location when the caller is dialing 911 from a cell phone. In some areas, the dispatch may receive the address of the cell tower the caller is connected to but not the exact address of the caller. In other areas, dispatchers may receive a geographic area, or sector, based on triangulation of the cell towers nearest to the cell phone. Therefore, it is of vital importance to ensure child-care-program staff know the physical address of their workplace.

The capabilities of emergency dispatch centers in the United States vary greatly and are constantly changing. Currently, some jurisdictions are testing or implementing systems that allow individuals to send text messages to 911. However, text to 911 is not available in all areas of the United States. Likewise, according to the Federal Communications Commission, many emergency dispatch centers are not equipped to receive photos and videos.

When a call comes in to 911, the dispatcher will pull up a script and will begin questioning the caller about the emergency. It is important to provide as much accurate information as possible, without guessing. Make sure to tell the dispatcher that the call is coming from a child-care program and that children are present. This information will greatly aid the responding officers. This is particularly true if the call is from a family child-care home or from a provider with after-hours care. Most first responders think of child care as day care and will likely assume that a program or building is closed after 5 or 6 p.m. Provide the dispatcher with the program's location and be as specific as possible. Also try to provide information about the shooter, if you know it. In some situations, shooters have attempted to change outfits and flee. If the shooter is visible, look for items and characteristics that cannot easily be changed, such as height, weight, and race. Also, look at what type of footwear the individual has on. Active shooters may attempt to change clothes, but rarely will they change their shoes.

Reasons the Response May Be Slowed

Alerting law enforcement as quickly as possible is important. However, many factors can slow the law enforcement response—all of which add up to the loss of valuable time. For example, sometimes people delay calling 911 while they explore or verify that the action is needed, or they may assume that someone else has already called. At the dispatch center, a high call volume may force the call system to place incoming calls on hold as it waits for a dispatcher to be free to answer. It may take time for the dispatcher to ask the caller for information and enter it into the computer system. In the event of a call from a cell phone, there may be a possible delay to be transferred to a different dispatch center if the call was routed to the wrong center. The dispatcher will have to locate the units closest to the emergency. Once a call has entered the system, there may be delays in law enforcement's response. The nearest officer may be on another call or away from her vehicle. Officers responding may be unfamiliar with the location, especially if they are from another jurisdiction. There may be confusion about what building, or what location inside the building, is experiencing the emergency.

SAMPLE 911 CALL

DISPATCHER: 911, what is your emergency?

CALLER: Hello, I'm hearing gunshots. I'm worried we have an active shooter in the area.

DISPATCHER: Okay, I understand. We will get help on the way. Can I please have your name and the address that you are calling from?

CALLER: My name is Susan, and I'm calling from Children First Kids Academy. We have 100 kids here and are located at 111 South Street. We're located inside of the church building on the lower level, and our entrance is in the very back of the building, off of the parking lot on the left side by the playground.

DISPATCHER: Okay, I have that information. Tell me what you are seeing or hearing now.

CALLER: I heard a bunch of loud bangs at the opposite end of the hallway, by the chapel and classroom 7. We have our classroom numbers posted on our outside windows.

DISPATCHER: Are there any injuries?

CALLER: Not in my room, but I did hear yelling and screaming down the hallway.

Ways to Aid Law Enforcement and Reduce Response Time

Active-shooter events are one of the highest priority calls that law enforcement agencies receive. Typically, these will be "all call" situations, meaning any available units in the area will respond as quickly as possible. This will likely mean that police officers from multiple jurisdictions will respond to an incident. In such an instance, different police cars, uniforms, and even some plain clothes officers will arrive at the scene. These individuals may or may not be familiar with the child-care facility. Therefore, it is incumbent on child-care programs to aid law enforcement and implement procedures, such as the following, that will help reduce police response time.

- Ensure that the building's address is clearly visible.
- Mark external doors and windows so that individual classrooms can be readily identified from both inside and outside the building.
- Install signage to indicate where the child-care program is located, if on a large campus or in a large building.
- Make sure that staff are wearing identification.

Often, child-care programs that operate within businesses or faith-based and congregation buildings can be hard to find. Simple signage indicating where the child-care program is located can greatly aid responding officers and cut down on time spent trying to locate your program. Staff should wear T-shirts, aprons, lanyards, or identification badges that identify them as employees or volunteers who belong in the facility. While police will be thorough in ruling out threats, having identification for staff can help this process move along more smoothly. In addition, staff members will be used as a resource by the responding officers and will also likely be asked to play a role in family reunification.

For programs with multiple classrooms, having classroom identification numbers inside and outside is a tremendous help. This provides the officers with a reference point—"the shooter is by classroom 3"—which can be identified from both inside and outside.

> **"Each classroom having exterior windows shall have the classroom number affixed to the upper right-hand corner of the first and last window of the corresponding classroom. The numbers shall be reflective, with contrasting background, and shall be readable from the ground plain at a minimum distance of fifty (50) feet."**
>
> —Recommendation from the Sandy Hook Advisory Commission

6

Conducting Drills

It is important to conduct drills to help staff and children understand what to do in the event of an active-shooter event. However, it is equally important that the drills not traumatize the people who are involved. We want preparation, not panic—trained, not traumatized.

Consider some examples of how we can get a preparedness message out without being scary. One great example is the airline industry. When we fly, we recognize that the mandatory safety briefing is designed to provide us with knowledge on what to do in an emergency. The airlines do not show pictures or videos of planes catching fire or crashing, even though that is exactly what they are preparing us for. In much the same way, we want to conduct active-shooter drills in a way that provides the information but does not traumatize children or staff.

There is little research regarding the effects of emergency-preparedness drills on children; however, a study by researchers Elizabeth Zhe and Amanda Nickerson examined emergency-response drills in elementary school children. They found that there may not be any effect on anxiety levels if drills are properly conducted. Early childhood professionals already possess the knowledge of how best to keep the children in their care calm and to ensure they are not scared. So for emergency-preparedness training, tapping into existing knowledge and coupling that with proven techniques is important.

The Extended Parallel Processing Model, originally developed by researcher Kim Witte, is a way of examining how threats motivate a person to act. This model takes into consideration the severity of a threat, a person's susceptibility to that threat, and a person's efficacy in responding to the threat. In short, when the threat is perceived as high risk but a person believes that he is able to effectively respond to the threat, then he is more likely to take action. Conversely, when the threat is high but a person believes that he is not prepared, or if he is not aware of the threat, then he is less likely to take action. The basic premise is that by conducting regular training that provides solutions, empowers employees, and gives them advance knowledge, employees are more likely to take protective action during a threat.

The topic of an active shooter is undoubtedly unique and has the potential to be more anxiety-producing than a fire, tornado, or earthquake drill. We must acknowledge this fact and ensure our actions are purposefully calculated so that we do not cause unnecessary or inadvertent trauma or anxiety to our staff and children. There are several considerations that must be taken into account before conducting active-shooter drills.

- **First, unannounced active-shooter drills should never happen.** Never. There is simply too much that could go wrong with conducting a surprise drill. Consider some of the things that could potentially happen: A passerby could mistakenly assume that the drill was a real-life incident. Some individuals may not understand it is a drill and unnecessarily suffer extreme stress. Law enforcement could be called and respond to what they believe is a real incident. A passerby who has a concealed-carry permit could rush in with a weapon in an attempt to help. None of these situations would result in a positive outcome, and some could even damage the reputation of your business or lead to potential legal liability. The National Association of School Psychologists and the National Association of School Resource Officers concur, stating, "Armed-assailant drills should never be unannounced.

  Unannounced drills can cause unnecessary fear and strong emotional and physical reactions." An *unannounced drill* means that those leading the drill say there is an active-shooter event with the intent to have staff respond, but fail to let staff know that they are responding to a fictitious scenario. As a result, the participants believe the incident is real. Any active shooter drill should be announced so that those participating do not experience emotional trauma, and so that any passerby does not think an actual event is occurring. Further, it is recommended to let your local law enforcement agency and dispatch center know that you are conducting an active-shooter drill. These entities can be reached through their non-emergency telephone numbers and may even offer to provide on-site support for your drill. Use plain language to announce, "This is a drill," multiple times at the start and throughout an exercise as a best practice to avoid confusion or distress.

- **Second, adults should understand what needs to happen in training and drills before attempting to incorporate children into any kind of drills or other planning efforts.** We do not want an adult participating in her first drill when children are present. Your staff should convene and practice response options ahead of time before introducing these concepts to children. This allows for consistent messaging and also allows the adults to have a solid understanding of the actions they are going to take during the drill.

  For instance, if you are going to practice hiding in a bathroom with the children, first consider how many children could safely fit in the space, how you will explain the activity to them in an age-appropriate way, and what activity or tactic you will use while in the bathroom to practice being quiet with them. If you plan to use a glow ball to keep the children quiet, you will want to test turning off the lights, turning on the glow ball, and having an adult stand outside the bathroom to ensure no light can be seen from outside the room. Adults planning and practicing an exercise like this first will help make it more effective and useful when incorporating children into the planning.

- **Third, these response options should be implemented gradually.** For instance, think back to the first time you conducted a fire drill. It was probably a chaotic situation at best. Once children learned what to do and what your expectations were, the drills likely got much better. We want to apply the same concept in this setting. Progression is key.

  For example, let's say that you have identified your bathroom as a hiding spot. A first step would be to introduce the hiding spot to the children: "Let's play a game and see if we can all fit in the bathroom. Hey, look! We all fit in here!" Then, a few days later, try it again, but this time try to stay in the bathroom for a little bit longer. Encourage the children to stay quiet: "I bet we can be so quiet in here that Ms. Smith will not be able to hear us!" You can use incremental steps to build upon the drill each time. Eventually, you can try to turn off the lights and have the children remain quiet. Not only is this a good exercise for active-shooter preparedness, but it also may help some students become more comfortable with the dark.

- **Fourth, avoid the use of the term *active-shooter drill*.** It may needlessly scare children. Drills should reinforce learning in a calm environment. They provide an opportunity to set expectations for children.

WAYS TO MESSAGE DRILLS TO CHILDREN

- **Hide and Seek:** This could indicate to children that they should find a hiding place quickly and quietly where others will not be able to easily find them.
- **Uninvited Guest or Animal on Campus:** For older children, they could understand the concept of an uninvited guest or someone to stay away from and appropriately go to a designated hiding area or place.
- **Bees to a Beehive:** For younger children, the beehive could be a designated hiding location such as a bathroom or hidden play area.
- **Cat and Mouse:** Let children know that there's a cat looking for them and they are the mice. They must hide quickly to win the game.

All emergency-preparedness trainings and drills should be treated seriously. They are an opportunity to practice our techniques, validate our assumptions, and identify any potential issues or shortcomings in our emergency plans. Effective drills should be conducted routinely and should provide an opportunity for staff to consider escape paths, rendezvous points, identification and use of hard corners, emergency communication procedures, techniques to keep children calm and quiet, and family reunification. Such planning and practice will provide a richer learning experience and help staff become more comfortable with these concepts and response actions.

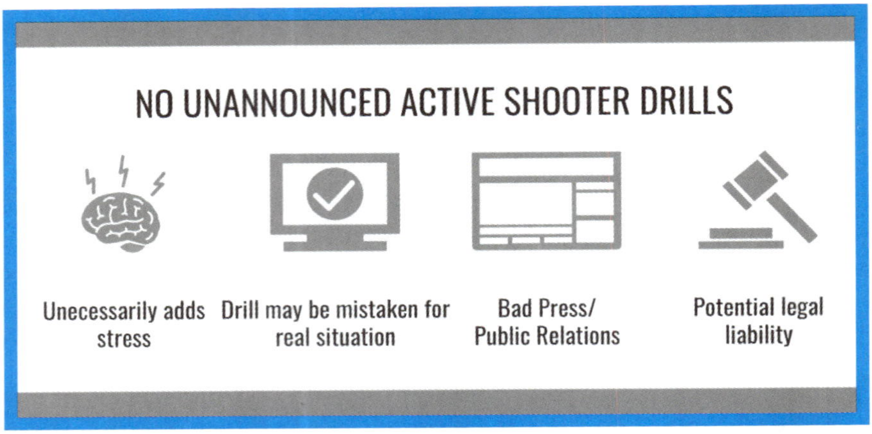

Conclusion

On an everyday basis, early childhood professionals provide a nurturing, caring, and educationally rich environment for our children. As those who are entrusted to care for our youngest and most vulnerable, we have a duty to create an environment that is as safe as possible.

The steps outlined throughout this book provide a foundation to help make your program more secure. This book should serve as a resource and a reference for this topic. To be most effective, you are encouraged to develop a comprehensive strategy that includes the following components:

- Training for all staff
- Engagement with local community groups, such as police, emergency management, fire, and EMS
- Regular drills and exercises
- Engagement with parents and updates to the parent handbook
- Routine reevaluation of plans, strategies, and tactics
- Regular review and updating of emergency plans, including the incorporation of lessons learned from drills and exercises, as well as real-world events

Life is constantly changing, and we are constantly learning. It is important that efforts are made to ensure your plans and drills do not become stagnant and out of date. Each drill is an important opportunity to test your plans and identify any shortcomings. Continued engagement, practice, and reevaluation will ultimately benefit your program and help ensure your plans are well vetted, practical, and reality based.

I hope that you have found this book helpful. I greatly appreciate all you do each day to keep children safe and hope that this publication has provided you with some additional strategies to enhance your security.

Tools and Resources

The US Department of Homeland Security website offers information on the Run, Hide, Fight approach. Find it at https://www.ready.gov/active-shooter

US Department of Education, Office of Postsecondary Education offers *The Handbook for Campus Safety and Security Reporting*, 2016 Edition. Find it at https://www2.ed.gov/admins/lead/safety/campus.html

A video on active-shooter preparedness by the US Department of Homeland Security is available at https://www.dhs.gov/cisa/options-consideration-active-shooter-preparedness-video

The Department of Homeland Security has developed a sample Emergency Action Plan form to help people prepare for active-shooter incidents. The downloadable form is available at https://www.dhs.gov/sites/default/files/publications/active-shooter-emergency-action-plan-template-112017-508.pdf

The Active Shooter Event: Quick Reference Guide by the US Department of Homeland Security is available at https://www.dhs.gov/publication/active-shooter-pamphlet

The US Department of Homeland Security booklet *Active Shooter: How to Respond* is available at https://www.dhs.gov/xlibrary/assets/active_shooter_booklet.pdf

The National Association of School Psychologists and the National Association of School Resource Officers have developed "Best Practice Considerations for Schools in Active Shooter and Other Armed Assailant Drills." You can find this at https://www.nasponline.org/resources-and-publications/resources-and-podcasts/school-climate-safety-and-crisis/systems-level-prevention/best-practice-considerations-for-schools-in-active-shooter-and-other-armed-assailant-drills

The Santa Ana School Police have posted a video on YouTube.com called "SAUSD Run Hide Fight (Elementary School)." It demonstrates and walks you through these three responses. Find it at https://www.youtube.com/watch?v=R6YjDmAnafQ

The ALiCE Training Institute offers active-shooter preparedness training. For information, see their website at https://www.alicetraining.com/

The Institute for Childhood Preparedness offers in-person and online active-shooter training designed specifically for early childhood settings. For more information, see https://www.childhoodpreparedness.org

Sesame Street in Communities offers a wealth of information in its Resources for Traumatic Experiences. Find it at https://sesamestreetincommunities.org/topics/traumatic-experiences/

The University of Missouri has developed the Disaster and Community Crisis Center. The website offers disaster and community crisis information, as well as information on trauma and building resilience. Find it at: https://dcc.missouri.edu/

The US Federal Bureau of Investigation, Office of Partner Engagement website offers information and statistics on its Active Shooter Resources page, available at https://www.fbi.gov/about/partnerships/office-of-partner-engagement/active-shooter-references

References and Recommended Reading

American Academy of Pediatrics, American Public Health Association, and National Resource Center for Health and Safety in Child Care and Early Education. 2011. "Standard 9.2.4.3: Disaster Planning, Training, and Communication." *Caring for Our Children: National Health and Safety Performance Standards; Guidelines for Early Care and Education Programs.* 3rd ed. Elk Grove Village, IL: American Academy of Pediatrics; Washington, DC: American Public Health Association. https://nrckids.org/files/CFOC3_updated_final.pdf

Blair, Pete, and Katherine Schweit. 2014. "A Study of Active Shooter Incidents in the United States, 2000–2013." Texas State University and Federal Bureau of Investigation, US Department of Justice. Washington, DC. https://www.fbi.gov/file-repository/active-shooter- study-2000-2013-1.pdf/view

CBS News. 2018. "Sandy Hook Shooter's Writings and Belongings Must Be Released to Public, Court Rules." CBSNews. https://www.cbsnews.com/news/sandy-hook-shooter-adam-lanza-writings-and-belongings-must-be-released-to-public-court-rules/

Center on the Developing Child. n.d. *In Brief: The Science of Early Childhood Development*. Cambridge, MA: Center on the Developing Child at Harvard University. https://46y5eh11fhgw3ve3ytpwxt9r-wpengine.netdna-ssl.com/wp-content/uploads/2007/03/InBrief-The-Science-of-Early-Childhood-Development2.pdf

Center on the Social and Emotional Foundations for Early Learning. n.d. "Tucker Turtle Takes Time to Tuck and Think." Resources: Practical Strategies for Teachers/Caregivers. http://csefel.vanderbilt.edu/resources/strategies.html

Centers for Disease Control and Prevention. 2017. "Deaths and Mortality." Life Stages and Populations: Death. https://www.cdc.gov/nchs/fastats/deaths.htm

Centers for Disease Control and Prevention. 2017. "Heart Disease Facts." Heart Disease. https://www.cdc.gov/heartdisease/facts.htm

Chavez, Nicole. 2018. "This School District Is Arming Students with Rocks In Case of A Shooter." CNN. https://www.cnn.com/2018/03/24/us/pennsylvania-school-students-armed-rocks-trnd/index.html

Child Care State Capacity Building Center. 2017. *How States and Territories Can Plan for Recovery*. Washington, DC: Early Childhood Training and Technical Assistance System, Administration for Children and Families, US Department of Health and Human Services. https://childcareta.acf.hhs.gov/sites/default/files/public/emergency_preparedness_response_and_recovery_planning_to_recover_0.pdf

Child Trends Databank. 2019. "Suicidal Teens." ChildTrends. https://www.childtrends.org/indicators/suicidal-teens

CNN. 2019. "Virginia Tech Shootings Fast Facts." CNN. https://www.cnn.com/2013/10/31/us/virginia-tech-shootings-fast-facts/index.html

Columbine Review Commission. 2001. *The Report of Governor Bill Owens' Columbine Review Commission*. Denver, CO. http://www.policefoundation.org/wp-content/uploads/2018/07/Columbine-Governors-Commission-Report.pdf

Commonwealth of Virginia v. Grafton William Peterson, Administrator of the Estate of Erin Nicole Peterson, Deceased, et al. 2013. Supreme Court of Virginia. 749 S.E.2d 307. https://caselaw.findlaw.com/va-supreme-court/1648245.html

Connecticut State Police. 2012. *After Action Report of the Connecticut State Police: Newtown Shooting Incident December 14, 2012*. http://lmgcorporate.com/wfsb/news/csp_aar.pdf

D'Agostino, John. 2019. "Deadly Masterminds Put Us on Defensive." *Observer Today*, May 3. http://www.observertoday.com/news/page-one/2019/05/deadly-masterminds-put-us-on-defensive/

Ergenbright, Charles, and Sean Hubbard. 2012. "Defeating the Active Shooter: Applying Facility Upgrades in Order to Mitigate the Effects of Active Shooters in High Occupancy Facilities." Thesis. Monterey, CA: Naval Postgraduate School. https://calhoun.nps.edu/bitstream/handle/10945/7337/12Jun_Ergenbright_Hubbard.pdf

Federal Bureau of Investigation. n.d. Active Shooter Resources. Washington, DC: FBI Office of Partner Engagement. https://www.fbi.gov/about/partnerships/office-of-partner-engagement/active-shooter-resources

Federal Bureau of Investigation. n.d. Quick Look: 250 Active Shooter Incidents in the United States From 2000 to 2017. Washington, DC: FBI Office of Partner Engagement. https://www.fbi.gov/about/partnerships/office-of-partner-engagement/active-shooter-incidents-graphics

Federal Bureau of Investigation. 2016. *Active Shooter Incidents in the United States in 2014 and 2015*. Federal Bureau of Investigation, US Department of Justice. https://www.fbi.gov/file-repository/activeshooterincidentsus_2014-2015.pdf/view

Federal Bureau of Investigation. 2017. *Active Shooter Incidents in the United States from 2000–2016*. Washington, DC: Federal Bureau of Investigation, US Department of Justice. https://www.hsdl.org/?abstract&did=806895

Federal Bureau of Investigation. 2018. *Active Shooter Incidents in the United States 2016–2017*. Washington, DC: Federal Bureau of Investigation, US Department of Justice. https://www.hsdl.org/?abstract&did=810325

Federal Communications Commission. 2019. 911 Wireless Services. Washington, DC: Federal Communications Commission. https://www.fcc.gov/consumers/guides/911-wireless-services

Federal Emergency Management Agency. 2019. Children and Disasters. Washington, DC: FEMA, US Department of Homeland Security. https://www.fema.gov/children-and-disasters

Federal Trade Commission. 2015. *Start with Security: A Guide for Business: Lessons Learned from FTC Cases*. Washington, DC: Federal Trade Commission. https://www.ftc.gov/system/files/documents/plain-language/pdf0205-startwithsecurity.pdf

Fretz, Rachel. 2007. *Lessons Learned at Virginia Tech Shooting*. Report from the 9th Annual Technologies for Critical Incident Preparedness Conference and Exposition presented by the US Departments of Justice, Homeland Security, and Defense in San Francisco, CA, November 2007. https://www.policeone.com/school-violence/articles/1473536-Lessons-learned-at-Virginia-Tech-shooting/

Friedman, Matti. 2007. "Holocaust Survivor Killed in Va. Shooting." *The Washington Post*. http://www.washingtonpost.com/wp-dyn/content/article/2007/04/17/AR2007041701224.html?noredirect=on

Frosch, Dan. 2014. "'Active Shooter' Drills Spark Raft of Legal Complaints." *The Wall Street Journal*, September 4. https://www.wsj.com/articles/active-shooter-drills-spark-raft-of-legal-complaints-1409760255

Green, Anthony, and Donna Cooper. 2012. "Auditing the Cost of the Virginia Tech Massacre." Center for American Progress. https://www.americanprogress.org/issues/guns-crime/reports/2012/04/12/11382/auditing-the-cost-of-the-virginia-tech-massacre/

Gun Violence Archive. 2019. Past Summary Ledgers. Gun Violence Archive. http://www. gunviolencearchive.org/past-tolls

Hawa, Sharon. 2014. "Children Separated by Disasters: Reunification Challenges and Resources." *IAEM Bulletin* 2014(6): 24–25. https://www.iaem.org/portals/25/documents/Hawa-Article-IAEM-Bulletin-June2014.pdf

Hays, Holly. 2019. "Noblesville Shooter Was Youngest Active Shooting Suspect of 2018, FBI Says." *IndyStar*, April 11. https://www.indystar.com/story/news/2019/04/11/noblesville-shooter-youngest-active-shooting-suspect-2018-fbi-says/3439081002/

Health Communication Capacity Collaborative. n.d. *The Extended Parallel Processing Model: An HC3 Research Primer*. http://www.healthcommcapacity.org/wp-content/uploads/2014/09/Extended-Parallel-Processing-Model.pdf

Healthline. 2016. "Why Are We Afraid of Being a Victim of a Mass Shooting?" Healthline. https://www.healthline.com/health-news/why-are-we-afraid-of-mass-shootings#3

Healthline. 2019. "What Are the 12 Leading Causes of Death in the United States?" Healthline. https://www.healthline.com/health/leading-causes-of-death#cancer

Heightman, A. J. 2019. "Safety Considerations at Active Shooter and Mass Casualty Events." Address to the National Emergency Medical Services Safety Summit, March 27, Denver, Colorado. https://www.jems.com/articles/2019/03/where-is-a-j-heightman-national-ems-safety-summit.html

Herron, Arika. 2019. "Teacher That Stopped Noblesville School Shooting Criticizes Active Shooter Training Bill." *IndyStar,* April 23. https://www.indystar.com/story/news/politics/2019/04/23/what-noblesville-teacher-jason-seaman-says-about-indiana-active-shooter-training-bill/3544365002/

Huriash, Lisa J., Scott Travis, and Tonya Alanez. 2018. "What Went Right on the Second Floor in Parkland?" *Sun-Sentinel*, December 31. https://www.sun-sentinel.com/local/broward/parkland/florida-school-shooting/fl-ne-parkland-second-floor-htmlstory.html

Lentini, Rochelle, B. J. Vaughn, and Lise Fox. 2005. *Tucker Turtle Takes Time to Tuck and Think: Scripted Story Tips*. Teaching Tools for Young Children with Challenging Behavior. Tampa, FL: University of South Florida. https://iod.unh.edu/sites/default/files/media/Project_Page_Resources/PBIS/a5_handout_tucker-turtle-takes-time_muscott.pdf

Leser, Kendall, Julie Looper-Coats, and Andrew Roszak. 2019. "Emergency Preparedness Plans and Perceptions among a Sample of United States Childcare Providers." *Disaster Medicine and Public Health Preparedness,* April 1–5. https://www.ncbi.nlm.nih.gov/pubmed/30940263

Marjory Stoneman Douglas High School Public Safety Commission. 2019. *Initial Report Submitted to the Governor, Speaker of the House of Representatives and Senate President*. http://www.fdle.state.fl.us/MSDHS/CommissionReport.pdf

May, Ashley. 2018. "Messages Reveal Boy Planned a School Shooting Worse than Parkland but Instead Killed Himself." *USA Today*, March 2. https://www.usatoday.com/story/news/nation-now/2018/03/02/messages-reveal-13-year-old-boy-planned-school-shooting-worse-than-columbine-but-instead-killed-hims/388256002/

Mears, Bill. 2013. "Virginia High Court Dismisses Virginia Tech Mass Shooting Lawsuit." CNN, October 31. https://www.cnn.com/2013/10/31/justice/virginia-tech-shooting-negligence-lawsuit/index.html

Murgado, Amaury. 2013. "Quicker Response to Active Shooters." *Police*, October 16. https://www.policemag.com/341042/quicker-response-to-active-shooters

National Association of School Psychologists. 2017. "Best Practice Considerations for Schools in Active Shooter and Other Armed Assailant Drills." National Association of School Psychologists. https://www.nasponline.org/resources-and-publications/resources-and-podcasts/school-climate-safety-and-crisis/systems-level-prevention/best-practice-considerations-for-schools-in-active-shooter-and-other-armed-assailant-drills

National Association of School Psychologists. 2019. "Mitigating Psychological Effects of Lockdowns." National Association of School Psychologists. https://www.nasponline.org/resources-and-publications/resources-and-podcasts/school-climate-safety-and-crisis/systems-level-prevention/mitigating-psychological-effects-of-lockdowns

National Coalition Against Domestic Violence. n.d. "National Statistics." NCADV. https://ncadv.org/statistics

National Safety Council. n.d. "Odds of Dying." National Safety Council, Preventable Deaths. https://injuryfacts.nsc.org/all-injuries/preventable-death-overview/odds-of-dying/

Norman-Eady, Sandra. 2007. Sex Offenders' Residency Restrictions. Connecticut General Assembly. https://www.cga.ct.gov/2007/rpt/2007-r-0380.htm

Office of the Child Advocate, State of Connecticut. 2014. *Shooting at Sandy Hook Elementary School: Report of the Office of the Child Advocate.* Office of the Child Advocate, State of Connecticut. http://www.ct.gov/oca/lib/oca/sandyhook11212014.pdf

Osborne, Mark, and Bill Hutchinson. 2018. "Survivor of Florida Yoga Studio Shooting Thanks Man Who Confronted Killer: 'He Saved My Life.'" *ABC News,* November 5. https://abcnews.go.com/US/dead-including-shooter-gunman-opens-fire-yoga-studio/story?id=58938747

Pazniokas, Mark. 2013. "Prosecutor's Report Provides Details, Not Answers, On Sandy Hook." *The CT Mirror,* November 25. https://ctmirror.org/2013/11/25/prosecutors-report-provides-details-not-answers-sandy-hook/

Pegues, Jeff. 2019. "Virginia Beach Shooting Survivors Say Training Helped Save Lives." CBS Evening News, June 3. https://www.cbsnews.com/news/virginia-beach-shooting-survivors-say-active-shooter-training-helped-save-lives/

Peterson, Jillian. 2019. "How to Prevent School Shootings." TEDx Hamline University. YouTube. https://www.youtube.com/watch?v=Ox1dJDs451o

Peterson, Jillian, and James Densley. 2019. "School Shooters Usually Show These Signs of Distress Long Before They Open Fire, Our Database Shows." The Conversation. http://theconversation.com/school-shooters-usually-show-these-signs-of-distress-long-before-they-open-fire-our-database-shows-111242

Police Executive Research Forum. 2014. *The Police Response to Active Shooter Incidents*. Washington, DC: Police Executive Research Forum. https://www.policeforum.org/assets/docs/Critical_Issues_Series/the%20police%20response%20to%20active%20shooter%20incidents%202014.pdf

Porter, Noriko. 2012. "[USA] High Turnover among Early Childhood Educators in the United States." Child Research Net. https://www.childresearch.net/projects/ecec/2012_04.html

Ropeik, David. 2018. "School Shootings Are Extraordinarily Rare. Why Is Fear of Them Driving Policy?" *The Washington Post*, March 8. https://www.washingtonpost.com/outlook/school-shootings-are-extraordinarily-rare-why-is-fear-of-them-driving-policy/2018/03/08/f4ead9f2-2247-11e8-94da-ebf9d112159c_story.html

Sandy Hook Advisory Commission. 2015. *Final Report of the Sandy Hook Advisory Commission*. Sandy Hook Advisory Commission. http://www.shac.ct.gov/SHAC_Final_Report_3-6-2015.pdf

Santa Ana School Police. 2017. "SAUSD Run Hide Fight (Elementary School)." YouTube. https://www.youtube.com/ watch?v=R6YjDmAnafQ

Sedensky, Stephen J. III. 2013. *Report of the State's Attorney for the Judicial District of Danbury on the Shootings at Sandy Hook Elementary School and 36 Yogananda Street, Newtown, Connecticut, on December 14, 2012*. Hartford, CT: Office of the State's Attorney, Judicial District of Danbury, State of Connecticut. https://portal.ct.gov/-/media/DCJ/SandyHookFinalReportpdf.pdf?la=en

Seewer, John. 2018. "Boy Who Shot Himself Planned Attack on Jackson Middle School, Police Say." *The Enquirer*, March 2. https://www.cincinnati.com/story/news/2018/03/02/police-boy-who-shot-himself-planned-attack-jackson-middle-school/388073002/

Schurgin O'Keeffe, Gwenn, and Kathleen Clarke-Pearson. 2011. "The Impact of Social Media on Children, Adolescents, and Families." *Pediatrics* 127(4): 800–804. https://pediatrics.aappublications.org/content/127/4/800.full?sid=4add2868-6c2b-4513-908a-509af13c2b53

US Department of Education, Office of Postsecondary Education. 2016. *The Handbook for Campus Safety and Security Reporting, 2016 Edition*. Washington, DC: US Department of Education. https://www2.ed.gov/admins/lead/safety/campus.html

US Department of Homeland Security. 2018. *Active Shooter: How to Respond*. Washington, DC: US Department of Homeland Security. https://www.dhs.gov/xlibrary/assets/active_shooter_booklet.pdf

US Department of Homeland Security. 2018. "Human Resources or Security Professional." US Department of Homeland Security. https://www.dhs.gov/human-resources-or-security- professional

US Department of Homeland Security. 2017. "Active Shooter Workshop Participant." US Department of Homeland Security. https://www.dhs.gov/active-shooter-workshop-participant

Virginia Tech Review Panel. 2007. *Mass Shootings at Virginia Tech April 16, 2007, Report of the Review Panel*. https://scholar.lib.vt.edu/prevail/docs/VTReviewPanelReport.pdf

Witte, Kim. 1992. "Putting the Fear Back into Fear Appeals: The Extended Parallel Process Model." *Communication Monographs* 59(4): 329–349.

Zhe, Elizabeth, and Amanda Nickerson. 2007. "Effects of an Intruder Crisis Drill on Children's Knowledge, Safety, Anxiety, and Perceptions of School Safety." *School Psychology Review* 36(3): 501–508.

Index

A

D

E

F

G

H

I

L

M

N

O

P

R

S

T

U

V

W

Z